Asian Americans: Reconceptualizing
Culture, History, Politics
Franklin Ng, series editor

ASIAN AMERICANS

RECONCEPTUALIZING CULTURE, HISTORY, POLITICS

edited by
FRANKLIN NG
CALIFORNIA STATE UNIVERSITY,
FRESNO

A GARLAND SERIES

重新找回中國的根

CLAIMING CHINESE IDENTITY

ELIONNE L.W. BELDEN

GARLAND PUBLISHING, Inc.
New York & London / 1997

Library of Congress Cataloging-in-Publication Data

Belden, Elionne L.W.
    Claiming Chinese identity / Elionne L.W. Belden.
        p.   cm. — (Asian Americans)
    Includes bibliographical references and index.
    ISBN 0-8153-2991-1 (alk. paper)
    1. Chinese Americans—Texas—Houston—Ethnic identity.
2. Chinese Americans—Cultural assimilation—Texas—Houston.
3. Chinese American teenagers—Texas—Houston. 4. Chinese
American families—Texas—Houston. 5. Language schools—
Texas—Houston. I. Title. II. Series.
F394.H89C513 1997
305.895'107641411—dc21
                                                    97-31033

Printed on acid-free, 250-year-life paper
Manufactured in the United States of America

For Rick and Zoé

Contents

Preface

This book is a meditative vehicle. I've not set out to write a definitive ethnography about immigrants to Houston, Texas—nor specifically about Chinese immigrants, nor specifically about Chinese immigrants at the Evergreen School. This meditative vehicle is neither a map of knowledge, nor a guide to action, nor intentionally entertainment. Rather, I have privileged functionalism over formalism, evocation over presentation and representation, extemporaneous experiences over precisely represented dialogue.

My work is about the dependent opposition of same/different by which we can make possible an understanding, application of identity in the consideration of any group. While my agents in this book are first generation Chinese immigrants (primarily those in the most literate class of the Evergreen School, and their parents), there are several considerations I make in defining the essential idea of identity: a functionalist application; ghosts and memory; the differences between palimpsest and pentimento, and the lasting marks the latter makes; a sense of rootedness and of belonging; Bakhtin's distinctions between the epic and the novel; the coming together of sameness in the face of so much that is different to the immigrants about Houston; and other immigrants who have either tried to invent their own traditions, have developed neuroses about their inherited identity, or have tried through nostalgia and illusion to create a presence of an absence. In the course of reading meaning (which is instrumental, purposive, and expressive) into this work, it is my intention that the reader not fall victim to the Procrustean syndrome by which only a narrow ideal (or definition of a people) is acceptable.

Acknowledgments

I cannot recall a time in my life when, given to think about how people lived their lives and the *doxa* they held for themselves, I wasn't aware of the opposition same/different. As I increased my years and my knowledge, it became clear that identity exists only by opposition to that which is different. It is by comparisons—that is contingencies/dependencies—that we make judgments and establish perimeters. I gratefully acknowledge the teachings of Stephen A. Tyler and his luminous writings for refining my thinking on this subject and particularly for taking a significant portion of five years of his life to get me through a doctoral program at Rice University. I know that in his intellectual generosity he appreciates my cognitive functions of language (the said as well as the unsaid) and forgives me, his student, any inadequacies in my instrumental expression.

The students, the faculty, and the administration of the Evergreen School allowed me, and Other, to be a presence in their lives for over a year. For an even longer period of time, many countless additional members of the Houston Chinese community were gracious and patient with me; in particular, I would like to thank Wei Wu, Joanne Lin, and Tai Chen. All these people not only diligently attempted to answer my copious questions, they also invited me to participate with them in many Chinese community activities and offered opinions and information of further subjects and ideas about which it had not occurred to me to ask. I am also grateful to Joanne Lin for teaching me the scholarly art of Chinese calligraphy and for providing the artwork on the title page.

George E. Marcus and Richard J. Smith set fine standards of academic excellence, and I thank them for lending their help to my dissertation while I was at Rice. I particularly appreciate the detailed thought Rich gave to my experiences, interpretation, and expression of my study group in the Chinese community.

There are ghosts that advance and retreat in our lives. Ghosts underlie and connect each of us to our pasts, root each of us, and serve as touchstones if not the actual bedrock to structure which is so profoundly necessary to one's life. I carry with me the ghost of my maternal grandmother who instilled in me when I was very young a love and respect of our French heritage and a celebration of the risks which immigrants take in their pursuit of new life elsewhere. Her grandmothers who immigrated from France in the nineteenth century had the same affect on her. In turn, I am influencing my daughter in this manner. Through these efforts, none of us have ever really left France; and it has been only since my grandmother's lifetime that we have enjoyed an ease with which we can often physically return to France as well.

Finally, but by no means least, I thank my husband Rick and my daughter Zoé for their love and support at all times and in all places. I returned to graduate school when Zoé was barely two-years-old, and I am painfully aware that she has been forced to share me with my nagging need for increased education and academic accomplishment. Her words have become a mantra for me: "I love you, Mommy. You can do it!" It is they who should share credit for my achievements, and it is I who must be solely responsible for my shortcomings.

E.L.W.B.
July, 1997

List of Abbreviations

ABC	American-Born Chinese
ESL	English as a Second Language
FOB	Fresh Off the Boat
HISD	Houston Independent School District
KMT	Kuomintang
NAFTA	North American Free Trade Agreement
SAT	Scholastic Aptitude Test
TAAS	Texas Assessment of Academic Standards
WASP	White Anglo-Saxon Protestant

Note on Transliteration

Throughout this book, I use the *pinyin* romanization system for transliterating all Chinese terms. Where names of people and places are well known in the public domain by another form or have been employed specifically by my informants in another form, I have retained that spelling. An example is Sun Yat-sen rather than Sun Yixian.

Claiming Chinese Identity

Same and Different

I
Introduction

The same never coincides with the equal, not even in the empty indifferent oneness of what is merely identical. The equal or identical always moves toward the absence of difference, so that everything may be reduced to a common denominator. The same, by contrast, is the belonging together of what differs, through a gathering by way of the difference. We can only say "the same" if we think difference. It is in the carrying out and settling of differences that the gathering nature of sameness comes to light. The same banishes all zeal always to level what is different into the equal or identical. The same gathers what is distinct into an orginal [sic] being-at-one. The equal, on the contrary, disperses them into the dull unity of mere uniformity.

> Martin Heidegger
> from ". . . .Poetically Man Dwells. . . ." in
> *Poetry, Language, Thought*

How do we know what is the same, unless we know the different? How can we recognize difference and yet expect it to conform to the exacting standards of Procrustes' bed, measuring its suitability and dooming whatever failed to be the same? How can we talk about identity (*idem*—the same) without comparing it to that which carries meaning in an entirely different direction (differ, *dis*—apart + *ferre*—to carry)? How can we know people are what they are without knowing what they are not?

This book is written to create an understanding of identity as revealed through my studies of a group of Chinese immigrants to Houston, Texas. These people are consciously *claiming* their identity, shaping it and refining it out of the immigrants' cultural traditions and history, and reifying this claim in opposition to their encounter with a new Western milieu of unbridled personal independence. It is in exploring the opposition of sameness and difference that an understanding of identity emerges, an understanding which is applicable—*necessary*—if one is to adroitly recognize that identity exists to the exclusion of difference.

Identity is a mutable, essential idea held in common, signified by agreement, by sameness and often manifested as some recognizable difference; but there is no particular essence, no particular quality or fundamental nature to which we can point and call "identity." What we are seeking to identify by name is not equivalent to the essence of that object, Heidegger says. The subject we question has a relationship to its essence but never in the sense of genus or *essentia* (Heidegger 1977:305-317). For example, "when we are seeking the essence of 'tree', we have to become aware that what pervades every tree, as tree, is not itself a tree that can be encountered among all the other trees," (ibid.: 287). Likewise, what is identified as essential about Chinese immigrants in Houston in no way points to a sameness about all Chinese.

The people in my study call upon their past to reformulate their present; and in so doing they *respond* to their historical consciousness as well as to quotidian realities. But they do not *correspond* to other Chinese. So, while the Chinese I studied respect the foundations established by their ancestors, they have adjusted and accommodated themselves to the circumstances in which they find themselves today, far removed from the China of the past. For them, being Chinese is an ethnic cultural consciousness and not a geopolitical identity. For them, China is more a concept than it is a place. But, most importantly, my work revealed that Chinese youth being raised with uncompromised attitudes toward honoring the family, maintaining personal humility, and developing Chinese literacy skills are a people set apart—by their choice—from a larger world: a world they see as being less harmonious for lacking much of the integrity, balance, and family values the Chinese have fiercely honored for so long.

Pluralism still has no place among some Chinese—in particular, among my study group. The Chinese have successfully resisted the social and cultural traits of the dominant West to which other immigrant groups here have succumbed. Conformity and unity have long been prized in Chinese society, and these people have strength in their large numbers of like-mindedness and abundant cultural markers in Houston. So it is not surprising that what Alan Wachman says of contemporary Chinese and Taiwanese living on Taiwan is equally applicable to the people in my study: "Collective consciousness rather than idiosyncratic expression is still valued highly," (Wachman 1994:56). My aim here is to present a thematic exposition of Chinese identity that is indicative not only of how some Chinese are accommodating that collective consciousness to living in Houston but, more importantly, how that Chinese identity is formed and lived in opposition and contingency to the milieu of Western difference. Moreover, while the Chinese are my agents in creating the dependent opposition of same/different, my work is about the essential characteristic of identity; and while I will make herein comparisons of other immigrants' experiences, my intention is not to compare cultures but rather to make possible an understanding, an application of identity in the consideration of any group.

For nearly everyone of the Chinese immigrants with whom I worked and studied, Houston was their first experience with being the minority member of a community. Within that group, there were a few other Chinese who had lived outside of mainland China or Taiwan in smaller metropolitan areas before coming to Houston; and for them there was a preparedness for thinking of themselves as the Other, rethinking themselves by comparison and contrast (i.e., opposition) with those people who had no Chinese identity. But once in the large metropolis of Houston, *vis-à-vis* a dominant culture far different from their ethnic sameness and from their family- and culturally-ingrained traditions, I found that everyone in my study resolved through a great deal of Chinese community effort to create a new style of being Chinese that fit more appropriately and conveniently with life in their new setting. But this does not mean they believe they are compromising their identity as Chinese. They honor the legacy of Confucian values, and they believe the individual exists in the context of his family. For them, being Chinese in Houston entails a conscious resistance of assimilating to a society which they consider lacking in family values and "right behavior." Yet, they have no qualms about appropriating the educational, economic, and recreational opportunities here.

While I was researching the identity (newly-formed as well as traditionally-maintained) of these Chinese immigrants, a subtext of racial attitudes emerged and became an unavoidable component of how I saw their experience of identity formation among Others in Houston. It is quite obvious as I detail the personal stories of some Chinese and my own purview of other scholars' research that attitudes toward their own ethnicity *vis à vis* other local racial groups (mine included) are among the factors in the Chinese accommodating their lives here. Undoubtedly, in encountering difference, the Chinese understand their sameness: their culture and their ethnicity. Attending to racial differences are, quite simply, a means of setting themselves apart and "to level what is different into the equal or identical," (Heidegger, as quoted in the epigram). There are those who would examine my work and conclude not only that the Chinese are racist but also that they are just one of another group of immigrants to the United States who in their synchronistic settlement into the "American way of life" provide yet another voice to the American discourse on racism. This is obviously the unfortunate thinking of someone who has fallen into the soporific lull of repetitive acamagicians pulling the same old tired trick with a false-bottom hat.

If there is to be a discourse in anthropology which examines the multiple ways in which immigrant groups communicate their thoughts or opinions, especially by words, then it is imperative that each group recognize in themselves as well as in the Other the ascription of difference; because by that very antithesis of sameness there exists a different perspective. Though thought is represented in language, people who learn English, for example, as their second or third language (which is the case for everyone in my study group) must conform to the signs that express it (cf. Tyler 1978:5). Language, "by virtue of its fundamental role in representing thought to ourselves and others, is an odd sort of necessary impediment to thought. Our knowledge of the world, given in our concepts about the world, is represented by the language we speak. Each language is the repository of the collective experience of a people, expressing their accumulated concepts and their organization of knowledge. Arbitrary discriminations of grammar and vocabulary constitute a world view—a distinctive way of understanding the world. A language then, is both a system of knowledge—an object of the understanding—and, as the actualization of analytic reason, the means of knowing. As a consequence, language is the limit of rationality and the limit of the world (Wittgenstein 1922). It prescribes what is spoken of and how one speaks of it," (Tyler 1978:5).

In choosing to make this application of Tyler's commentary on the form and function of linguistics, I hasten to add that from their position as newly-arrived outsiders the Chinese are not imbued with the same nuances and forms of expression (in this case, regarding racial differences and opinions about those differences) as that of other Houstonians. Indeed, in Amy Tan's words, the traditional expression of Chinese thought in "Chinese words are good and bad this way, so many meanings, depending on what you hold in your heart," (Tan 1995:29). Just as Tyler distinguishes speech from language, the former "by which is intended both speaking and writing, is the outer representation of the inner form of language," adding that speech "is not language, it is only the appearance of language, the physical means by which individuals make manifest the presence in themselves of that universal and transcendental form which is itself a sign of their humanity," the Chinese I studied often chose English words to distinguish themselves from others, to describe themselves as set apart in culture and philosophy from non-Chinese (Tyler 1978:5). The easiest way for the young Chinese to do this was to employ much of the same vocabulary "Americans" use but not necessarily for the same purpose. Quite simply, racial remarks made by the Chinese in most cases were made to distinguish themselves in an opposition signifying interdependence of subjectivity and objectivity rather than their mutual antagonism (cf. Tyler 1978:4). I believe the racial remarks made by the Chinese were meant to set themselves apart (granted, in an expression of pride in themselves and their long-standing traditions and fully-imbued sense of their culture); but the remarks were never a means of privileging themselves in an effort to relegate, even harm, Others.

While my work centers on how a group of Chinese have created a collective identity of ethnic and cultural consciousness, it is also imperative to recognize a distinctiveness between the younger Chinese in my study (ages 13-18) and their parents and Chinese teachers. I found that a sense of communal identity for the young Chinese immigrants is tied more to the place where they currently reside than to their place of origin; there is no sense of loss of the China of their past, because they carry with them what they remember—and are reminded of by their families and Chinese teachers—leaving behind. Further, they are willing and prepared to contribute to the Houston of the present.

But for the parents there is still a strong emotional tie to an ancestral place defined in terms of patrilineal relations. They are torn between allegiance to their parents who still believe in the "old ways" and who often still live in Taiwan, and establishing a new authoritarian order of family attitudes governing them and their children in their lives in the West. Therefore, a consideration as we develop an understanding of these people's identity is that rather than allowing present circumstances to rewrite them (assimilation), they have rewritten their interpretation of their cultural past to fit the present (accommodation). Said another way, they do not sacrifice their past and their values in order to reformulate themselves for the present.

The focus of my studies is the 16-year-old Evergreen School, the city's second-oldest Mandarin Chinese language school, which has a student enrollment of 450. It was established by the Houston Chinese Women's Association with the expressed purpose of teaching Chinese language and culture, and with the additional implicit purpose of making friends within the Houston Chinese community. In the early days of its operations the school met on the Rice University campus which is centrally located in the city, across the street from the museum district, the city's most popular park, the famous medical center, and only a few minutes drive from the downtown business district and the first significant Chinatown which is smaller and less patronized than the second Chinatown in southwest Houston. As attendance at the school grew, new locations were sought to accommodate the interest.

And now every non-holiday weekend Evergreen holds its Sunday classes on the Chinatown-area campus of Strake Jesuit High School, a Catholic boys high school from which Evergreen has leased space since 1991. The campus, located on Bellaire Boulevard near the corner of Gessner Drive in southwest Houston, is a spacious piece of land characteristic of the sparse, lean architectural design of the 1960s. Its numerous one-story light-colored brick buildings punctuate large grassy areas and are connected to each other by equally-simple metal-roofed breezeways which are supported by unadorned steel poles flanking the concrete sidewalk. The building foundations are level with the street and level with the parking lot so that, except in one area where the ground seems to decline for drainage, one walks straight into the building instead of having to lift one's self up and into the (exalted) place of learning. The purpose of the educational facilities, therefore, is rather straight-forward. The interior design of nearly all the classrooms replicate one-another: fluorescent lighting; white ceiling tiles; vinyl floor tiles; a television monitor; two chalkboards and one or more bulletin boards; windows spanning one wall of each classroom; and, of course, a crucifix on the wall just inside the classroom door. Except for the distinctive cross at the entrance of the school and the crucifixes inside, the campus' simplicity is an interesting non-interfering statement—and, therefore, support—to providing a milieu where the complex work of identity (re)formation is undertaken.

The majority of my fieldwork was with the most literate students in a classroom where the grade levels ranged from seventh through senior year in high school. Gender representation in this group was about 60 percent female and 40 percent male. The teacher was male, and nearly all of the visiting speakers were male. The administration was female, and members of its staff visited the class from time to time for the purpose of distributing awards to the students or providing the teacher with paperwork. The classes were conducted almost wholly in Mandarin, and English was exceptional when certain traditional Chinese phrases or expressions (such as those used in philosophical discussions) were unfamiliar to the students. All of the students spoke English quite well, though there were some students (here in the West for about a year) with somewhat diminished skills and hesitancy in initiating a conversation with me in English. I have acquired some

Chinese reading ability, but I speak so very little of the language.[1] Therefore, all the conversations I had with my informants were conducted in English.

My research was initiated in a friendly and informal way by a friend who invited me to the Chinese school where she was substitute teaching one day. There was no overt reason for her invitation other than she wanted my company in the classroom; and knowing well that I was a doctoral student in anthropology at Rice University and that I had been to Asia on several occasions, she thought I would find the afternoon "immersion" in Chinese culture rather interesting. I did. So much so that from that day and for the next 15 months I continued nurturing that interest, formalizing it into my fieldwork.

Everyday I "went into the field," I was leaving my home in the center of this large densely-populated metropolitan area and driving twelve miles to another world where Asians were the dominant group and I was the Other. Within walking distance of my house, there is a popular inner-city commercial area patronized by many cultures and races drawn to its bookstores and coffee shops selling trendy styles of caffeine consumption; boutique clothing shops and restaurants; shops with "wilderness" equipment; shops that sell fine wine; and a theater that shows foreign "art" films. Nearby is also the residential and commercial area known to be the place where the gay community and social activists congregate. Not far away is the museum district and the campuses of Rice and St. Thomas universities. In the other direction from my house is a street leading to downtown Houston where "shotgun houses" for poor black people still stand, still inhabited by poor black people. In the opposite direction from the row houses is the River Oaks neighborhood with its large residential statements and eponymous country club which costs $50,000 to join. Leaving all this, I would travel south along one or the other major parallel traffic routes of Shepherd Drive or Kirby Drive until I took the feeder road to Highway 59-South, get onto this congested freeway that bi-sected one of my travel arteries, accelerate to keep pace with the seemingly hell-bent drivers around me, and keep going until I was outside the highway loop (metaphorically and geographically) from my normal life. I would exit at Sharpstown Mall (a commercial statement whose existence still bewilders me, although I came to understand from my informants that the mall provided a social arena for kids who couldn't otherwise see each other after school), turn *west* onto Bellaire Boulevard and drive several more miles to the Chinese school.

My inner-city life is lived among large oak trees whose age (50-60 years), size, and arrangement along streets and in yards testify to a long-ago planned community that remains standing and growing. But once I am on Highway 59 heading away from my verdant vistas I am immediately slapped into a gray concrete consciousness that never brightens; only a few decades earlier this southwest part of town was pasture home to cows and horses, and no gardens had been sculptured for the bovines' benefit. Traveling along multi-lane Bellaire Boulevard at speeds exceeding the posted limit are more small Japanese cars than any other place I have ever seen in Houston. It always seems to me that most of these vehicles (80-90 percent?) are driven by Asians and that the same percentage of cars nearly always has one (usually at least two) other passengers. This is so different from the part of town in which I live and from the expansive Galleria where I sometimes shop; and I surmise that car trips in this working-class, far-southwest area are planned for economy of time and gasoline—something not always considered if one is in the tony Galleria shops or nearby area to pick up a cashmere cardigan at Neiman-Marcus, select a ball gown at Saks Fifth Avenue, peruse the silver at Tiffany & Co., or shop at Cartier for something to embellish oneself!

This southwest Chinatown (only about five to 10 minutes by car from the Galleria) where the Evergreen School is located is a neighborhood which was created in the early 1960s as Houston's home to the fashionable American vision of new suburban convenience: new schools, new shopping, new homes, new streets. The hallmark of this *modus vivendi* was a sprawling development called Sharpstown. Houston was booming then. The Vietnam war was in full force a short while later, and the great influx of southeast Asians that would follow the collapse of fighting efforts in South Vietnam was yet to come. The Chinese would arrive in Houston in greater numbers later. Meanwhile, principal travel arteries such as Bellaire Boulevard, Gessner Drive, and Harwin Drive were in place; and aggressive, speculative retail developments mushroomed along these streets, crowded one after the other. There appeared no end to the success stories as Houston continued to boom through the 1970s. Then what had appeared to be a vehicular economy which could continue soaring to new heights proved to be just a bubble.

It was the energy industry (my reason for moving to Houston more than 20 years ago) that burst that bubble. Long the greatest single employment arena for Houstonians, its collapse against a row of domino-game relations leveled the economy here. As people lost there jobs, spending was reserved for essentials like groceries, home mortgage payments, and less expensive goods and services. Soon much of the retail space in this southwest area was vacant, and the formerly fashionable vision of suburbia became an eyesore. Banks began to fail when loans from the former retailers and developers went unpaid: foreclosures and repossessions dramatically increased the banks' inventory of unleased and unwanted retail space in place of cash receipts, and depositors could retrieve only as much as the U. S. government had insured.

For some time, this southwest eyesore remained untreated. The property, although aesthetically unattractive, was still available—and on a lower cost basis. "But who around here would possibly want it or could possibly make it a success?" many people wondered. Yet the notion of immigration is synonymous with looking for opportunity. What Others here in Houston believed was a problem, the immigrants from east and southeast Asia saw as that opportunity. What followed here along Bellaire Boulevard and the other neighborhood streets in the 1980s was a critical mass of Chinese businesses which not only attracted other Chinese to this area but precluded competing visions of a new Chinatown area built from scratch (as was attempted and failed in another part of southwest Houston). The older downtown area could no longer offer the same economics of revitalization: the buildings and warehouses were just too old, and the area was too small; old houses and buildings would have needed to be acquired and razed, adding substantial capital to the project. What the Chinese did then was to claim an area for their own and revitalize it. They did not merely approach the new Chinatown as an inheritance with which they could just "make do." Rather, they took something tarnished that once was shiny, took something old that once was new, and accommodated it and themselves to a story which unfolds as "Twice upon a time. . ."

Just pass the monolithic mall, as one is barreling westward down Bellaire Boulevard, the businesses are greater in number and smaller in size. Strip center after strip center, nearly all to the north of the road, identify themselves in Asian languages as well as in English. First come the smaller countries: Vietnam and Cambodia. Then farther down there are some tri-lingual signs in Vietnamese, Chinese, and English. Then one begins to see overwhelmingly large numbers of Chinese. The street name signs begin to change, also. To my knowledge, Chinese street signs here and on the other side of downtown Houston, east of where the city government and many tall office buildings are crowded together, are the only other-language municipal signs erected in all of Harris County.

If one parks (because one cannot walk about here except within the context of walking from store to store in a length faced by a parking lot) and goes into one of these centers, the smells and chatter and products on the shelves or signs identifying the goods and services sold will differ from any other part of mainstream Houston. There are few non-Asians here, so if one is accustomed to eating with a fork, it must be requested in many of the restaurants. There may be an English-language newspaper vending machine, but one has to search quite awhile to find it. And the grocery stores devote a large amount of space to selling woks, bamboo skewers, and Chinese-motif dinnerware (usually plastic like one is served on in the family-owned and -run restaurants). Expect the fowl for sale to be cooked and lacquered red and hanging by their heads. And expect to see crustaceans and seafood so "fresh" that they are crawling in their wooden crates and swimming in their tanks. There are many of these centers similarly arranged but disconnected, so one must unpark and drive down the street to the next area in order to shop there, too.

Up and down Bellaire Boulevard the sights are the same. Sometimes there is a Kentucky Fried Chicken or other type of fast food franchise, but the real flavor remains Chinese. In some cases there is a concession in the name of an establishment that signals an attraction to non-Chinese. One such establishment was right next door to the Strake Jesuit/Evergreen campus, and sight of it always makes me laugh. It's name is FantAsia.

From the beginning, my physical place in the classroom was seemingly informal and friendly—somewhat accepted and unobtrusive—because I, a tall red-haired Wendy WASP type wearing her Brooks Brothers penny loafers and crewneck sweater over simple slacks, was being introduced to the class at the invitation of a Chinese woman with whom I was friendly. Her position as a mother of Chinese school students and as a teacher made her *the* authority in the classroom; the students were expected to accept me. They didn't have to like me, but they had to accept me into their environment. Fortunately, they liked me, and I liked them. Had there not been some mutual curiosity about our differences, surely my fieldwork would have been tiresome and troublesome.

Instead, much of my time in the field was conducted in the informal way I had formalized an earlier career in print and broadcast journalism. However, there were many times in my earlier life as a journalist when I had to finish a story at a frenetic pace to be on the air or to make the morning press deadline. But in this case, I had a more relaxed pace when I was with my informants. I began my place in the Chinese classroom and in the Chinese community as a quiet observer of speech, body language, and the way the structure of relationships as well as the structure of individual behavior was played out. I carried a small notebook, pencil, and eraser that by their minimalist size seemed less obtrusive, less a means of separation from me and my informants. Of course, I continued to research Chinese history and customs and glean information informally with Chinese friends so that I could in turn knowledgeably approach my informants. For example, rather than ask a parent or a student if there were any traditional Chinese celebrations they observed here in the West, I wanted to be able to ask specific questions such as, "Do you celebrate Double 10 (This is Chinese independence day which commemorates the end of the empire in 1911; it is celebrated October 1 on mainland China and October 10 on Taiwan.)?" and "Do your grandparents participate in the August Moon Festival (This is a tradition which is thousands of years old and is held during the brightest moon of the harvest time. Because the Chinese calendar is lunar, there are sometimes two Augusts. Fall, 1995 was such a double occurrence.)?" I believed from the very beginning of my fieldwork that much of the success I would hope to have in presenting a thematic exposition of Chinese identity—moreover, creating an understanding of sameness and difference—lay in my having a rapport with my informants. Early on, I accomplished this by sitting among them—never apart—and being available to the students to help them with their schoolwork (Helping them translate their Spanish homework and "make sense" of their American/European history homework were some of the things for which they became particularly indebted to me!). Talk of this helpfulness and genuine admiration they knew I had for their Chinese culture reached the homes, and I found I had an easier *entrée* to talking with the parents and other community members.

It is quite common for social science researchers to employ the devise of an interview schedule (cf. Stevens 1995). I abjured this from the very beginning of my fieldwork, because I feared such a formalized list of questions posed in the same way to every different informant would invalidate the friendliness I hoped to develop and, further, would blind me—or make me very myopic at best—to the unique contributions my informants could make from whatever individual experience and perspective each had. Questions had to be asked, though, regardless of the format. So, I undertook an intense education (reading and asking questions) about the China of their past and how much of China was with them today. I wanted to know how these people organized their lives and how that organization differed from my personal Western experience. I wanted to know what they held dear to them. I wanted to know their priorities and why they made them so. I wanted to know what was important to them. I wanted to know what they believed in. I wanted to know what *really* made them Chinese. So, I began by asking, "What is valued?"

NOTES

1. Early on in my field work I investigated Chinese language schools for non-Chinese speakers. Sadly, there are few opportunities in Houston to learn Mandarin unless one is enrolled in a several-months-long course which meets only three hours for the week, or hires a private tutor. Both these means were very inconvenient for my research schedule as well as for my family life. Finally, I found what I thought was my best option: a 10-week intensive course

offered through the Continuing Studies Program at Rice University. I paid my tuition in full and looked forward to the class. A few days before the course commenced, I received a telephone call from someone at the program's office explaining that the Chinese language class was canceled for insufficient enrollment: only a minimum of five students was needed to justify the class; yet only three of us had enrolled! My tuition check was returned, and I decided that my time would be better spent in research and in (English) conversation with my informants.

Evolution of Chinese Identity

II
What Is Valued?

Unquestioned submission to authority is a value that lies at the heart of the traditional Chinese value system and, ergo, culture (Pan, Chaffee, et al. 1994:218; Hsu 1981; Pye 1985:194). Yet, as my work examines, the normative status of virtues once honored in traditional China continue to undergo reformation. "America is the background to our *new* identity," a Chinese mother told me. "Our roots, our looks, tell us about ourselves. In one respect, our Asian features give us no other option to an identity. But being American is something we should know, too."

Cultural identity can no longer be confined to national boundaries alone (Chow 1993:92; cf. Smith 1994:287). There is no longer a traditional China in the form of identification with a clearly conceived Chinese nation; the configuration that once linked the people to the dimensions of a nation is now dismantled in the consciousness of those who have carved new lives for themselves overseas and yet identify themselves every much as Chinese as those who remain on the mainland.

In historical consciousness and cultural unconsciousness, kinship is *the* most salient feature, *the* most important relationship in Chinese culture and in the identity of being Chinese. In traditional Chinese culture, one's birth is *a priori* to one's membership in a clan; but on the mainland, especially, the acquired value of "loyalty to one's home village and pride in one's culture is vital to the structuring of one's existence, to the formation of one's identity," (Wang, L. 1991:195; cf. Liang Qichao in Arkush and Lee 1989:92). "The real Chinese individual has been, and still is, identified by reference to the greater

human context of his time," writes Robert Hegel in his exploration of
the Chinese literary self (Hegel 1985:6). The notion of independence—
of the singular self expressing thought and action without the origins,
consequences, and obligations to another self—does not exist among
the Chinese in their cultural traditions of society. And Lucian Pye adds
that even unquestioning acceptance of patriotism in the Chinese
political culture can be traced back to the denial of the self in favor of
the collectivity. "At one time the Chinese saw the collectivity as the
family or clan, but with modernization the collectivity became the
nation. This transition was more than a change in group identity; it
became exaggerated because Chinese culture, with its emphasis upon
being socialized in a larger group context—that is, within the extended
family or at least in a family in which a host of ancestors were looking
on—has made the Chinese self-conscious about an audience," (Pye
1985:194). As I will discuss in more detail when I review experiences
in the aforementioned individual classroom where I spent a great deal
of my time, there were a number of times during the course of my
fieldwork that I witnessed the uneasiness of students, in Houston for
only one to four years, who were called upon to promote themselves
before their high school peers and teachers. And I also observed these
same students' amazement when their age peers, in Houston nearly all
their memorable lives, did indeed get up before a class and speak
openly and proudly of their accomplishments and desires for
themselves (cf. Pye 1992:96-97). There was such a polite and obvious
distance between the two camps: the one so close to the Confucian-
inspired China of their upbringing, and the other the product of
socially-integrated Houston. The first camp was amazed at what they
considered the brazen attitudes of the others; the second camp was
understanding of the influences on the first camp's thinking but also not
totally at ease in socializing with them.

For more than two millennia, traditional Chinese society revolved
around clans, groups of individuals stemming from a common ancestor
and bearing the same surname. Scholars have continually commented
that "consequently, innumerable Chinese are related by consanguinity
and these clan relationships form the basis for preferred social
interaction, the extension of mutual aid and protection, and power
interrelations," (Lee 1960:135; cf. Arkush and Lee:11; cf. Pan, Chaffee,

et al.:19). Yet, as I address later, the lack of numerous and highly visible clan associations in present-day Houston is one means of illustrating the different issues affecting Chinese identity here.

Submission to some authority is, of course necessary in all countries; what differs from polity to polity is the exact nature of authority. "American culture has been characterized as emphasizing 'rationalism,' mastery of nature, and an orientation toward the future, all of which are opposite to a general conception of traditionalism," (Williams 1970 as quoted in Pan, Chaffee, et al.:233). The "American" traditions of the United States were erected not on the foundation of submission to European hierarchical systems but rather on the notion of overthrowing a government system whose tributary system was unidirectional toward the British king. The ancient Chinese phrase "Heaven is high and the emperor is far away *(Tian gao huangdi yuan)*, which expressed a feeling of village people that imperial intervention in their local society was remote, could easily be applied to Americans in the eighteenth century to describe their impatience with royal rule. Whereas deference to authority is central to the Confucian model, newer American and Western historical consciousness is fraught with, among others, technology which dilutes and deludes connection, saturating us with ways of conceptualizing the Human self and related patterns of social life (Gergen 1991); assertion of independence movements *(Declaration of Independence* 1776 and *Declaration of the Rights of Man* 1789); philosophical rationality (seventeenth century Descartes) and its challenges to its philosophical hegemony (seventeenth/eighteenth century Vico); departure from supreme religious temporal authority (the sixteenth century Protestant Reformation); and religious and ethnic persecution (the fifteenth century Inquisition).

Lynn Pan writes that to be "really and truly Chinese, it was commonly believed, one had to trace one's ancestry to the progenitor of the Chinese race," who was and is still held to be the Yellow Emperor Huang Di (Pan 1994:10). [Besides Huang Di, the Chinese also acknowledge Emperor Yan, or Yan Di better known as Shen Nong, who is mentioned whenever Chinese medicine is discussed. According to tradition, it was Shen who tasted the flavor of hundreds of herbs and created medicine and pharmacology (ibid.:11)]. "The theory that all

Chinese are ultimately descended from a common ancestor rest on the tradition that the Yellow Emperor had twenty-five sons, fourteen of whom were given distinct surnames by their father. It is dimly supposed that all Chinese names are derived in some way from the fourteen created by the Yellow Emperor, and contriving to demonstrate a connection to these has kept clan genealogists busy for centuries," (ibid.).

It is uncertain how many surnames exist (estimates have run from a few hundred to less than 5000), but it is absurd to assume that all those bearing the same surname share a common origin. Rather, the traditional importance of the name lies in the superordination of the clan (Lee 1960:135). Prior to the end of the last imperial rule in 1911, China recognized a person first by the dynasty under which he lived; obviously, this inextricably bound up one's personal identity in the facts of family and geographic origins (Hegel:5). Consider, for example, the superordinate position of the clan name as someone is known in society: it is Dr. Sun (surname) Yat-sen instead of Dr. Yat-sen Sun; placed uppermost, the surname soon quickly establishes kinship and perhaps clan geographical placement.

Of course, a common name and geographical distribution is an easily discerned acknowledgment of someone's physical place in society; but the more far-reaching means of identity is the social and economic organizations and the ways in which one is positioned in a network of relationships (*guanxi*) (Ambrose 1991). The obligations and duties in kinship relationships, for example, will invariably rank in patrilineal order with filial devotion being the most requisite and admired duty of a family member. "It entails unquestioned obedience of the son to the authority of his father during—and after—his father's lifetime (Pan, Chaffee, et al.:21). But "contrary to the popular conception of unidirectional control, this dyadic relationship implies active contributions by both parties...This aspect of the father-son relationship is represented by the traditional phrase 'benevolent father and filial son,' a reciprocal system," (ibid.). Further, what Richard J. Smith has written of the Qing dynasty can broadly be applied to the family structure since at least the time of Confucius who nearly two thousand years earlier laid the foundation of the conception of kinship relationships: "The theme of family life (and social life generally) was subordination: the individual to the group, the young to the old, and females to males. Kinship terminology, which reflected specific status rights and nonreciprocal status obligations, was highly refined, with nearly eighty major kinship terms in general usage. . .In the absence of a well-developed system of protective civil or commercial law, kinship bonds of blood, marriage, or adoption were the closest and most reliable ties in traditional Chinese society, even when the relationships were rather far removed from the nuclear family," (Smith:86-87; cf. Pye 1992:91-97). In the main, families "were Confucian in content, emphasizing family values, community harmony, ritual, respect, and self-control," (Smith:91).

While *guanxi* remains a strong "feudal" element of Chinese culture (whose presence in communist China has threatened the formal and official ideological system of Marxism-Leninism), the importance of the self, however, should not be minimized (Ambrose 1991:63). Indeed, the Chinese concept *xiushen* (self-cultivation) is an imperative to construct one's self as distinct from the Other. Further, a network of relations *establishes* identity but does not *constitute* the identity of an individual, because a person plays singularly different roles in a multiplicity of relationships.

Chinese social anthropologist Fei Xiaotong has written that social relationships in China possess a self-centered quality which has been translated into the Western psychoanalytic term "ego" (Fei 1992). For Chinese, he distinguishes "between the group and the individual, between others and our own selves. How this line has been drawn in China traditionally is obviously different from the way it is drawn in the West. Therefore, if we want to discuss the problem of selfishness, we have to take into consideration the pattern of the entire social structure," (Fei 1992:61).

Fei metaphorically contrasts Western society as bundles of straw, with Chinese society as the ripples produced by a pebble thrown into a lake, or as a spider's web. The basic social units of the West are organized with distinct boundaries, he says (ibid.). His analogy is that after harvest, straw is bound into small bundles, and those small bundles are added to others, each turning into a larger bundle which eventually becomes a stack. The separate straws, the separate bundles, and then the separate stacks all fit together to form the whole haystack.

Like Western society, he says, the orderly composition of haystacks clearly defines the relationship of each unit to the organization. He concedes that an individual may join several organizations, and that it is impossible for a straw to be in several bundles at the same time; but his point is to promulgate what he sees as the pattern of personal relationships in Western (American) social life.

"Our [Chinese] pattern is not like [that]. Rather, it is like the circles that appear on the surface of a lake when a rock is thrown into it. Everyone stands at the center of the circles produced by his or her own social influence. Everyone's circles are interrelated. One touches different circles at different times and places," (ibid.:63). The kind of networks, then, that he describes are a system of identification, of notation. But the difference lies in the people who are covered by a network: they are not the same as those covered by another network, and the only thing held in common is the system of notation itself, each web of social relationships linked specifically to each person. "Each web has a self as its center, and every web has a different center," (ibid.).

The holistic cosmological views of traditional China and their modern analog in the universalism ascribed to Chinese Marxism identifies the Chinese individual by reference to the greater human context of his time (Hegel:6). "To ordinary Chinese, the traditional view of being at the center of existence has always been an important aspect of being Chinese," (Wu 1991:160). This view presents a deep-rooted sense of belonging—mostly in isolation—to a unified civilization which boasts several thousands of years of uninterrupted history. The "Middle Kingdom," as we in the West know China, is actually not an Orientalist term fabricated in the West.[1] Rather, my informants translate it from the Chinese *zhonghua*, which means the country (culturally) centered and implying that the peripheral countries surrounding China were populated by culturally inferior barbarians. (This is reinforced by the term *jingong*, which was the Chinese means of exacting tribute from these smaller, inferior peoples who were given a kind of "protection" or "deferment" from Chinese invasion.) "As might be expected, the Chinese historical record abounds with praise for barbarians who 'admired right behavior and turned toward Chinese civilization.' Such conduct accorded perfectly with China's self-image of cultural and moral superiority," (*wenhua you yuegan*) (Smith:138).

However, as stated earlier, there no longer exists the concept of being Chinese as concurrent with there being a clearly conceived Chinese nation. Those networks of perpetual cultural identity have been politically discredited and dismantled, moving the concept of identity away from nationalistic terms and more than ever into the realm of conscious ethnicity and emphasis on connections as instrumental culture. This is not to say there is no causality in the politics of historical mainland China which was once so influential to Chinese identity. Rather, as Heidegger addresses essence, causality, and instrumentality in "The Question Concerning Technology," cause is what has an effect on its consequence; a correct instrumental definition of something still does not show us that something's essence, but "wherever ends are pursued and means are employed, wherever instrumentality reigns, there reigns causality," (Heidegger 1977:289).

NOTES

1. I refer to Edward W. Said's term "Orientalism" which he describes in his work by the same title as originating in colonial language and being a term the "Orientals" would not have applied to themselves without outside influence (1978).

III

Historical Setting: Beginnings of the Chinese Diaspora

The first large numbers of Chinese came to Texas four years after the end of the Civil War (Chen and von der Mehden 1982:2). The January 22, 1879 issue of *Harper's Weekly* reports that 250 Chinese workers arrived opposite Council Bluffs, Iowa (enroute to Texas) and, seeing the impassable ice-packed Missouri River, disembarked their boats and passed over a plank walk laid across the icy river "carrying their baggage on poles balanced over their shoulders in true Oriental fashion," (*Harper's Weekly* 1870:53; cf. Chen and von der Mehden:2). These laborers traveled south from St. Louis by steamboat and passed through Houston shortly thereafter on their way to work on the Houston and Texas Central railroads (Chen and von der Mehden:5).

Chinese workers were highly instrumental in expanding the nation's rail system, and Texans were among those who considered the Chinese better and more industrious workers than other groups. Records from the period indicate that at one time there were as many as 3,000 men employed by the railroads (ibid.:2). But by 20 years later, local discrimination and national legislation sharply reduced that number. Still, some managed to become residents of the young city, and by 1880 the census records seven Chinese citizens, including the first Chinese American born in Houston: Lincoln Yuan who was born to an interracial family (Caucasian mother, Chinese father) (ibid.:4). "All of these first citizens were in the laundry business, an activity monopolized here by the Chinese in the late nineteenth century," (ibid.).

The nineteenth century was the age of great migrations all over the world, responding to uncertainty at home as well as creating disruption within the areas of resettlement. The Chinese who departed the mainland in masses did so against the backdrop of the stresses of overcrowding, violent internal conflict, Western penetration, and faltering imperial authority (Pan 1994:43-57; cf. Wachman:15). Reviewing this diasporic beginning is useful in creating an understanding of how the past can influence and even contour the present.

A long period of internal peace produced a phenomenal population explosion that increased the population from 150 million people at the beginning of the century to well over 400 million by 1850 (Pan:43; Schirokauer 1982:93). Lynn Pan tells us that "in a country where there had appeared no new kinds of material, technical or political improvement to absorb the proliferation of people, such numbers made for destitution, popular demoralization, corruption, apathy, and the breakdown of public order and personal morality," (Pan:43). The lack of an increase in productivity or resources comparable to the population growth was, however, not the only impetus to mass migration.

The Treaty of Nanjing concluded the first Opium War in 1842, and the Manchu court was forced to cede Hong Kong to Britain as well as open five treaty ports—Canton, Amoy, Foochow, Ningpo, and Shanghai—to foreign trade and residence. The next year after negotiations with the British, the Chinese endured similar demands from the French and the Americans (Schirokauer:89). Further, this era of military and capitalistic invasion by the West was coupled with dramatic insurrectionary movements, most notably the Taiping Rebellion of 1850-1864.

This most devastating domestic challenge was led by Hong Xiuquan, a bizarre Hakka convert to Old Testament Protestant Christianity who was driven by convictions that in his visions he had seen God; he also "met" Jesus and believed him to be his own elder brother (ibid.:94; cf. Spence 1996). Recasting Christianity into a familiar familistic mode appealed to Hong's Chinese audience. But Western Christian missionaries were horrified by this as well as by

Hong's Christianity emphasizing the Old Testament rather than the New Testament, and the Ten Commandments rather than the Sermon on the Mount. Becoming an itinerant preacher after being expelled from his village for smashing Buddhist and Doaist "idols" as well as Confucian tablets (because of his zealous militant interpretation of the first Commandment), Hong attracted the poor and miserable by holding out a vision of the "Heavenly Kingdom of Great Peace" (*Taiping Tianguo*), an egalitarian, God-ordained utopia (ibid.). "Millenarian religious beliefs, utopian egalitarianism, moral righteousness, and hatred of the [dominant] Manchus" were fused into a program of talented strategy and organization (Schirokauer:95; cf. Smith:184 and 277-278). Starting from their base in Guangxi, the Taiping forces swept across sixteen provinces and destroyed more than six hundred cities. Millions of people died in all in the fourteen years it took the imperial forces to quell the rebellion.[1] "Never before in the two hundred years of Manchu rule had the empire been so horribly ravaged," (Pan:44). It is against this backdrop of devastation that we see the scene set for the beginnings of the Chinese diaspora.

Chinese American sociologist Rose Hum Lee reminds us that the word "diaspora" is an equivalent of the Greek term for a nation, or a part thereof, separated from its own state or territory but existing within the boundaries of another nation; and the diasporic communities are known as preservers as well as perpetrators of their national culture (Lee 1960:53). The term has a special reference to Jews for reasons of their collective dispersion after the Exile, for those living outside of Palestine, and for Jewish Christians living among heathens. Jews lived in involuntary segregation in ghettos hemmed in by walls at the time of the Roman Empire; after that era it is uncertain whether the walls were erected (ibid.:54). But the mental vision of a distinct physical barrier remained and continued to exist as an emotional and mental reminder of what separated the diasporic community from the dominant group. Of great interest to me—as I will describe later when I will discuss in more detail what I heard during Chinese education programs and the conversations which I had with informants during the time of my fieldwork—the comparison of the historical Jewish experience of persecution, alienation, and life in segregated communities is made by some Chinese immigrants (to Houston) as a means to focus their more recent history of troubles for the Chinese youth and to create for them, among other things, a sense of pride in their past and distinctiveness as an ethnic group whose cultural identity once had definition concurrent with definitive national boundaries.

Understandably, the trauma of being different among the Other, of having suffered greatly among "their own kind" in their own land, has an empathetic quality to Chinese immigrants (and, or course, to other minorities among the dominant). In present-day Houston, immigrant communities most likely form as a time-honored recurrent theme of common unity (community). Inasmuch as economic status may determine a physical location, a site inhabited by like-minded people of same-language speakers who form an economic milieu and organize a social structure of ritual, symbols, beliefs, and decorum. I hasten to clarify that whereas immigrant groups in the United States (Chinese included) were once forced to live in ghettos, the involuntary segregation has given way to voluntary living as a group set apart by distinctiveness of language and culture.

The Chinese script is universally read, but the dialects speaking it are geographically diverse. Hence, for the early immigrants from mainland China there was a strong attachment to a Chinese village reified by the commonalty of its speakers. It followed that "grouping by dialect was the first and the most spontaneous of the characteristics of the overseas Chinese community, and the special sentiment of the emigrants for their home district was reflected in the remarkable network of native-place or dialect associations which they established in all places in which they settled [at first, along the southern coast of China]," (Pan:20-21). The pattern of interlocking loyalties and enmities between dialect groups, secret societies, and clans "could not be exactly replicated abroad, but the tendency to fission. . .survived the journeys across the seas. For all their regional separatism, though, the expatriate Chinese were completely united in their passionate attachment to their homeland," (ibid.:21).

Like the Jews, many of the Chinese in the vanguard of overseas settlement experienced a great deal of exploitation and cruelty. These were often "coolies" who many times did not survive; some remained abroad and, embittered by their encounters with non-Chinese, "became more determined to stand proud as Chinese. . .Confronted with so much discrimination, identifying with China and asserting one's Chineseness became common," (Wang Gungwu 1991:141-142). Yet, especially for the first Chinese who ventured overseas with the idea of returning after years of hard work and increased financial independence, one's hometown or village place (*xiang*) remained one of the most evocative words in the Chinese language, "far more emotive than its equivalents in English," (Pan:21). The best known of all Chinese poems is one that is especially popular among expatriate Chinese; it is written by the famous eighth-century Tang dynasty poet Li Po and ends with that significant word *xiang* (home):

> So bright a gleam at the foot of my bed—
> Could there have been a frost already?
> Lifting myself to look, I see that it is moonlight.
> Lowering my head, I dream that I am home.
>
> (as translated in Pan:21)

Scholars point out that the Chinese rootedness in his own native place and his intense dislike of leaving his *xiang* were part of the importance he attached to his family. Indeed, devotion to *xiang* could be interpreted as an extension of filial piety. The Chinese word *gen* (roots) carries meaning aside from its basic biological significance: it designates one's birth place, ancestral village, or nativity—"the source from which one derives one's personal identity," (Wang, L.:182). So it followed that a Chinese geographical entity called China—one's *zuguo* (ancestral nation or motherland)—was the basis on which many overseas Chinese once structured their existence and identity.

Before this great migration period, the use of *gen* was purely cultural; but later political and legal consequences caused the meaning of *gen* to undergo change as expatriates reevaluated their desire to return to "China." They brought with them what they remembered leaving behind. And their stories of village life and the formidable structure of familial duty influenced their children growing up American. Maxine Hong Kingston gives us the reaction of American-born Chinese children who, upon hearing about corporal punishment harshly administered to their relatives in China said, "We American children heard too [about who has the duty of setting a good example],

and resolved not to 'return' to China," (Kingston 1980:23). In another
passage of the same monograph, she relates the thoughts of a young girl
growing up in San Francisco; the child doesn't quite comprehend the
common Chinese sayings of her immigrant father, and dismayed she
thinks, "You only look and talk Chinese. There are no photographs of
you in Chinese clothes nor against Chinese landscapes. Did you cut
your pigtail to show your support for the Republic? Or have you always
been American? Do you mean to give us a chance at being real
Americans by forgetting the Chinese past?" (ibid.:14).

Assimilation, compromise, and accommodation are all issues that
have clearly affected Chinese immigrants (cf. Bernard 1974). Before
the collapse of the American-backed Nationalist regime of Chiang Kai-
shek in 1949, first-generation Chinese in the United States continued to
identify themselves as Chinese whose being was as much tied to one's
mainland *gen* as it was to the rootedness of family and extended
guanxi. Now, the social and cultural loyalty has shifted in diaspora; and
the issues of "adaptation" must be evaluated anew against a backdrop
which succeeds millennia of tradition on the mainland.

Certainly it is misleading to consider that all Chinese immigrants
left their homes with the intention of settling and living out their lives
elsewhere. (In fact, what immigrant from anywhere in the world
doesn't dream of going home eventually?) As early as the sixteenth
century when traders ventured beyond the coastal regions, they
remained "completely united in their passionate attachment to their
homeland. Seeing their stay abroad as temporary, many awaited the day
when they could return to their villages in swank after making good—
or, to put it in the Chinese way, 'go home in silken robes'," (Pan:21; cf.
Sung 1967).

As immigration increased in the nineteenth century, so did
significant numbers of Chinese who intended only to work a few years
on the "Gold Mountain" and return rich beyond their dreams (Siu
1987:108). These workers (whose large numbers were overwhelmingly
male laborers) with their sense of impermanence, their unwillingness to
integrate themselves into the host society, were often resented for their
lack of commitment to anything more than "being Chinese." The
Chinese Exclusion Act of 1882 no less endeared the Chinese workers to
this country. That infamous legislation specifically barred this group of

people who maintained allegiances to their own hometown communities, abjuring the identity of being "American."

The point must be made that unlike a number of other immigrant/exilic groups, the Chinese had no sense of liminality—of being at the threshold of a door leading to a new and better(?) life all the while wondering if what they came from wasn't the more appealing. This liminality of other immigrant/exilic groups defines itself in an overwhelming sense of nostalgia and attempts at simulating in a new milieu what was left behind. "The exiles create hybrid identities and syncretic cultures that symbolically and materially borrow from both the indigenous society and the new one to which they have relocated. Such a hybrid identity and composite culture is characterized by contradictions and instabilities of all sorts which drive the culture and keep it 'honest' in the sense of preventing nationalism, chauvinism, sexism, ethnocentrism, xenophobia, puritanismn, solipsism, or absolutism of any kind from hardening it into some putative and dangerous cohesiveness. Overreliance on liminality and on haggling for individual positioning, however, frustrates group solidarity, political agency, and social representation—all of which are necessary if the exiles, in Stuart Hall's terms, are to come into political representation (Hall 1988:27). Coiling back on the self by forming hermetic, if successful, ethnic communities does not automatically translate into political representation in the host society. On the other hand, if acculturation occurs and exile turns into ethnicity, then exile is likely to become a steady absence, an alluring memory, a romanticized notion. For those who are still in liminality, it is the threat of absence that drives exilic consciousness toward perpetual nostalgia," (Naficy 1993:17).

Hamid Naficy aptly addresses this in numerous publications and film work about Iranians in the West, exiles who miss the Iran of their pre-Khomeini and pre-revolution past, who find it physically difficult and emotionally wrenching to return to the Iran of the present. Naficy, who is counted among those displaced peoples and cultures the world over and, hence, counts himself among those in the liminal state, writes that "we experience the present as a loss or, as Baudrillard would have it, as a phenomenon that has no origin or reality, a 'hyperreality,' " (Naficy 1991:285). This double loss of origin and of reality gives agency to nostalgia as a major cultural and representational practice among the exiles. Nostalgia, of course, is not just a feature of exile, he reminds us. Rather, "it is a constituent part of human development and it serves to repair our discontinuous identities as both individuals and collectivities by appealing to origins and commonalties," (Naficy 1993:147-148). Further, Naficy says, attempts by these liminal people to restructure their lives in the host country with cultural practices and decorative arts in the exiles' homes are not so much *reproducing* Iran as *producing* a world made of signs: not just to entertain or to decorate in itself but to signify production or at least the possibility of meaning. "The meaning that is produced involves establishing both cultural and ethnic differentiation (from the host society) and cultural and ethnic continuity (with an idealized past of the homeland)," (ibid.:290).

Underlining this sense of liminality and nostalgia is a fundamentally interpsychic source expressed in the trope of an eternal desire for return—a return that is structurally unrealizable, Naficy asserts. He further reminds us that Freud speaks of homesickness as a longing for a return to the womb of the motherland, and Naficy quotes Jane Gallop from her work, *Reading Lacan* (1985): "If we understand the nostalgia resulting from the discovery of the mother's castration in this way, then the discovery that the mother does not have the phallus means that the subject can never return to the womb. Somehow the fact that the mother is not phallic means that the mother as mother is lost forever, that the mother as womb, homeland, source, and grounding for the subject is irretrievably past. The subject is hence in a foreign land, alienated," (Gallop 1985:148 as quoted in Naficy 1991:285; cf. Naficy 1993:147-153).

This sense of loss of the motherland is inapplicable to the Chinese immigrants then (as well as now). These early migrant Chinese workers intentionally came to this country for reasons clear to them; and they had every intention of returning to the China that, regardless of domestic unrest, had always existed in some comprehensible state. They became known as "sojourners," a term introduced by Paul C. P. Siu in his classic study, *The Chinese Laundryman: A Study of Social Isolation* (1987). Siu compared the sojourner, one who spends many years of his lifetime abroad—often in many countries—without ever becoming assimilated by his host nations, to the person he identifies as the bi-cultural marginal man who tends to seek status in the society of the dominant group. By contrast, Siu writes, "The essential characteristic of the sojourner is that he *clings* [italics mine] to the culture of his own ethnic group," (Siu 1987:299). The term "became a great favourite [sic] with writers on the immigrant Chinese, who used it in the mistaken belief that the sense of impermanence marking the sojourner was somehow uniquely Chinese," (Pan:106). Words often used to characterize these Chinese included outsiders, strangers, pariahs, outcasts, visitors, temporary residents—and worse, "parasites, arrogantly holding on to their peculiar culture, reserved mannerisms, and frugal living habits, incessantly siphoning off the host countries' national assets and resources," (Wang, L.:193). As the sojourners came with culture-bound notions, they perceived themselves as *huaqiao* (overseas Chinese) (ibid.:194; cf. Siu:2; cf. Wang Gungwu). Their tenacious hold on their acquired value of loyalty to their home village and pride in their culture was maintained in a clan association, native-place or dialect communities not unlike the Jewish *Landsmannschaft* where one could go to find relief from the American environment and re-immerse oneself in one's Chineseness (cf. Howe 1989:183-184). "The clan association was a home from home, and life for the uprooted immigrant was greatly eased by it. At its most practical it was a welfare agency and a settler of disputes; on a subtler level, and as an organizer of the rituals of ancestor worship, it assuaged the member's nostalgia for the old country, helped to perpetuate descent lines, satisfied the need for a sense of closeness to one's origins and prolonged one's memories of home. In a community always in danger of being diluted by forces in the outside world, the clan association served as an oasis of Chineseness," (Pan:113).

Today, more than 125 years after the first Chinese were seen arriving "in true Oriental fashion," Houston's Chinese population is among the largest in the United States, after the metroplex sites of San Francisco, New York, Los Angeles, and Chicago (numbering more than 30,000 in Harris County and neighboring counties, according to the 1990 U. S. census which is a 100 percent form on the basis of self-identification). The city is easily accessible by air (including an active international airport and immigration office) and highway systems; and its inland position only 50 miles from the Gulf of Mexico is nonetheless connected to the Gulf by a man-made navigation channel characterized by assiduous commercial shipping.

While Houston has never had a formal Chinatown similar to other U. S. cities such as San Francisco and New York in which families might work, socialize, worship, attend school, and live for years without ever leaving their Sinicized geographical boundaries, the city does have an older downtown quarter that never expanded much beyond a few square blocks of commercial activity, and the much larger enterprise in the southwestern part of the metropolis that encompasses miles of commercial frontage on principal streets.[2] This second and more vibrant Chinatown hosts cultural centers, language schools (including the Evergreen School), bakeries and grocery stores, restaurants, karaoke bars, book stores, places of worship, furniture stores, publication offices, and more. Presently, developers plans call for a new expansion westward and juxtaposed to this now well-established Chinatown which metamorphisized from the aforementioned abandoned neighborhood of the 1980s.

The first Chinese residents who established themselves in the downtown area remained there for several decades; and "in the 1930s and 1940s, many Chinese opened groceries in the black areas on Houston's east side," (Chen and von der Mehden:5). "These shops were both living and work places--the families' houses with the store. The lack of any Chinese ghetto in those years can be seen by the fact that the children of that early period graduated from three different high schools: San Jacinto, Austin and Sam Houston," (ibid.). This older area borders the east side of downtown Houston and is accessible to the performance arts centers, the city services and city government buildings, and to shopping areas. These shopping areas, however, remain far less commercially important compared with the highly-trafficked shopping arenas of the Galleria in southwest Houston, approximately six miles from the central downtown business district; FM 1960 which is a lengthy east-west strip of mostly commercial activity approximately 20 miles north of downtown (and several miles northwest of the principal airport, George Bush International Airport/Houston); and the Katy Freeway corridor which begins approximately two miles north of the Galleria, and extends from approximately six miles west of downtown, through aggressively developing residential as well as commercial areas on former pasture area toward Katy, Texas some 30 miles away. A north-south freeway system extends between the old Chinatown and the rest of downtown Houston; and while this is not a physical impediment for traffic flow, it remains a visual statement of this Chinatown being set apart, of this area remaining distinct by an imposed design. Interestingly, in the 1980s the City of Houston built a very conspicuously-designed massive convention center with the idea of attracting and hosting diverse groups and their equally diverse programs in Houston. The convention center flanks the same highway system which "separates" the older Chinatown from the rest of the just-described parts of Houston.

Although the clan associations were once camps of familiarity invaluable in the transition experience of the Chinese—regardless of whether one was a sojourner, a student, or an individual wishing to make a permanent home in the United States—these associations in Houston are now practically non-existent or are considered to be "more American than Chinese," as several of my informants opined. Family associations in Houston are known to have been active some 45 years ago; and nearly 15 years ago approximately a dozen such groups were recorded (Chen and von der Mehden:14). But when I posed the question to a number of my informants as to whether any of them had been helped by a clan association in their resettlement to Houston (A few of these Evergreen parents arrived here as long ago as 20 years.), none had either contact or knowledge that such an organization existed. "The only one (clan association) I know about is the Gee family (a Cantonese family name pronounced like "Jew" in Mandarin and commonly spelled "Chu" by my Mandarin-speaking informants)," a man in his 40s told me; "and I'm pretty sure that the people running it are third generation Americans."

I was surprised at this non-involvement response from every one of the people of whom I asked about the importance these organizations played in their own experiences of immigration. Yet, I was aware that most of their social experiences were with other Chinese, except in some matters relating to business.

When I asked about other associations that would bring them in contact with non-family Chinese, I had a much more positive response. One man from Beijing (where he was born and educated through graduate school) enthusiastically told me of his active involvement in an organization that brings professionals of Chinese descent together. He was particularly excited that this group included large numbers of first generation Chinese from the mainland, because since his arrival in Houston a few years ago he was dismayed to so often encounter the attitude among other Chinese here that the mainland Chinese and everyone else (primarily those from Taiwan) "just don't mix. We have so much in common in our heritage," he waxed philosophically (and, I thought, unrealistically).

"Yes, we have a common heritage of historical experiences and philosophical influences, particularly of family values. But there is a large philosophical distance between those of us from the China mainland and those of us from Taiwan. My best friend is from the mainland, and we can talk about anything except Chinese politics and the independence of Taiwan," a Chinese professor actively involved in Taiwanese politics told me. "Also, there is a whole generation lost to communism. We Chinese are so proud of our honor and values, our honesty and integrity. But there are also mainland Chinese well into their 40s [age] that are dishonest and selfish; they have no understanding of the values we were taught in school and in our homes before the communists ruled. I have no use for them. I remember one time one of these people called me in my office and tried to get me to lie, to do something dishonest. I put the telephone down and told my secretary I was closing the door for two minutes and that she would hear loud sounds, but that I was going to be okay. Then I picked up the phone again and screamed at him!" The time frame of this infamous man's generation reminded me of the stories of children publicly humiliating their parents, following the state's lead in turning away from Confucian values, and denouncing anyone who was not complying with the Maoist form of communist doctrine.

Another professional Chinese man from Evergreen who I knew to be very conscientious about participating in Chinese community activities told me about his involvement in the Chinese Chamber of Commerce. He seemed very excited to tell me that the organization brought together professionals from throughout the Chinese community, and its activities extend beyond Houston, he told me. "For example, when the NAFTA (North American Free Trade Agreement) treaty was signed, a delegation went to Mexico to encourage economic exchange with the people there."

"Did you know there was a group of Chinese living in Mexico at the early part of this century?" I asked him.

"No," he said, but he wanted to know more.

"Yes," I continued, "by the early 1900s when the Chinese Exclusion Act had taken hold, there were a number of local businesses who were advertising slogans like 'The Chinese Must Go.' So they did. To Mexico. Then when General John Pershing went to Mexico in pursuit of Pancho Villa, Chinese merchants there helped his troops to survive (as I had read in Chen's and von der Mehden's monograph), and he brought them back to the States as refugees." I then quoted to him from the same monograph, "Because of the Exclusion Acts, they could not become citizens; in fact, it took them over five years to gain permission to become legal residents. They earned their keep by helping to build the army and navy bases used during World War I."

"Oh, I didn't know that," he replied a little sadly. I will add that this man came to the United States unattached to any family or business here. He has since married another Chinese immigrant, and as I've learned more in the last two years about his life, I've observed him being more and more involved in a variety of Chinese community activities spanning arts, business, and education.

An obvious question to ask is, "Why are Chinese coming to Houston?" Twenty-five to 30 years ago, nearly all the people in my study group who were young adults at that time came to attend graduate school. Education is always assumed to be achieved and is never an option for the Chinese. Today, however, economic opportunity is the most cogent response to their being here. An informant who earned her Ph.D. among that earlier group in the late 1960s related to me a story that amused her about another friend with similar immigration experiences: "'I was just over at Joy's house,' the friend said. 'I couldn't believe it! Her house is twice as big as mine and she spent twice as much money for it! I've been here more than 20 years, and she's been here only six months!!' " My informant laughed and pointed out to her friend that the two of them had come here at first for different reasons and never became so concerned with quick financial achievement the way the younger generation had.

"The cost of living is lower here than it is on the west or east coasts of this country," an administrator of the Greater Houston Partnership answered as part of the reason for Chinese immigrants locating here.[3] "The business climate of those coasts was pre-established by Europeans. The Chinese have been on those coasts for a long period, too, compared with the newest Chinese immigrants. So, there is an established infrastructure that is difficult to fit into or to challenge. For example, if there is a well-established publishing company or banking enterprise in one of those areas, a new immigrant might be told, ' You can't come in here and operate our kind of business.' For that reason, the Chinese find Houston to be more opportunistic; there is a more open society here."

"Value anticipated and realized" is the most operative term I would apply to Houston being any kind of mecca for the most recent (since the mid-1980s economic bust) Chinese immigrants, although this non-Chinese Asian at the Greater Houston Partnership didn't describe their attraction to Houston in this term. Nonetheless, my observations over the last five to eight years and conversations about investments in real estate and businesses with some Chinese for the last five years have reified my suspicions to become theory and my theory to witness actualization. Representatives of the Chinese community in Houston have been very astute about developing formerly pariah-type locations, often paying cash for them during a time of otherwise high interest loan rates. As testimony to this, two years ago a Chinese informant proudly told me that several years earlier during a particularly depressed time in real estate prices, a group wanted to start another Chinese language school in the southwest part of the city. Rather than pay rent to a landlord, the Chinese pooled $100,000 to purchase a run-down apartment building they found they could easily convert to classrooms. The capital improvements, added to the initial price of the building, produced a property in very good condition that was still below area market prices. The area surrounding this property started to improve as other landlords and tenets—recognizing their Chinese neighbors' initiative—improved their property, too; and the continuing circumstances are that the property so astutely purchased and remodeled by the Chinese has proved to be a profitable investment.

Among the Chinese—about whom many might say are synonymous with the issue of frugality—comparison of one's wealth and how it is spent conjures several means of distinguishing themselves that differs markedly from the Western notion of wealth. Undoubtedly, Americans have never successfully shaken their British-inspired class-system notion that is distinguished by whether one is "well-bred" gentry with all the accompanying accouterments of money, land, education, and servants (A title and a roman numeral after one's name was lovely, too!). In this country, sadly, one's class is most often judged in financial terms and its manifestations (big businesses, big houses, fancy cars with fancy prices, pedigree pets, etc.); and we all can immediately think of at least one or two parvenus who want to buy their "class." But rather than comment on other Chinese's wealth in terms of the richer being "better," the Chinese in my study group (who varied from small business owners and civil servants to Ph.D. professors to international billionaire business men and women) never made derogatory remarks about someone else's ill or good fortune. The tone of comments about another's wealth was always in the context of awe and respect for the achievement and whether someone was clever and efficient. There was also a note in the speaker's voice of humility rather than jealousy: "Oh, I could never do that. Oh, he has been very smart. He took a lot of risks in selling in that new market, and he did very well." Or, "Did you see that new car she bought? That's my dream car. Oh, she must have spent a lot of money on that car. I can't afford that." This latter comment comes from a woman who recently spent more than $500,000 cash on a large new home and who with her husband earns more than $250,000 annually. Yet, her sense of frugality dictates that she never spend more than $20,000 for an automobile and that she drives it for at least 125,000 miles.

Another distinguishing point of Chinese and "Western" differences is their sense of physical place in a community. Generally, Americans are effectively buffered against exogenous cultural inroads (Few Americans watch foreign films or read other-language authors.), while nearly all Asian societies confront accelerating Western influences manifested most recognizably in media (Pan, Chaffee, et al.:233) Chinese are not so uncomfortable living among white Americans who have already informed the Chinese with the exported brand of

American culture. And with its lack of zoning and expansive commercial, educational, and cultural activities, Houston is a panoply of opportunities. But Robert Reich, former secretary of labor for the Clinton administration, made a distinctive error in specifying the "American community" in his book *The Work of Nations: Preparing Ourselves for 21st-Century Capitalism* (1991). Writing that there is "only one thing Americans increasingly have in common with their neighbors, and this. . . .is their income levels," Reich further suggests that the financial status and its outward manifestations is also closely tied to educational levels (Reich 1991:277). By his definition, any ethnic and social, religious and philosophical, and political differences that may be represented among the community are relegated while income levels are privileged as the determining factor to locating oneself in a "community." (Reich:276-278). A zip code, he seems to think, is a divining rod leading to a neighborhood of cookie-cutter mind-sets. Yet, except for the Fort Bend County area which is heavily populated by Asians, the Chinese in my study group live all over town not only to find the best value in home-purchasing, but more likely to locate themselves in an area of safety and in a good public school district.[4] Further emphasizing that finding a neighborhood where one seeks a comfortable social environment is less a determining factor in buying or renting a home than is the desire to live among those of perceived comparable "wealth," Reich says that most people "commute to work and socialize on some basis other than geographic proximity to where they sleep," (Reich:277). His appraisal is simply inappropriate to Houston where real estate agents are quick to point out to prospective buyers that children live in the neighborhood, that parks are nearby, that churches, temples, and mosques are nearby, that the closest hospital is (x) blocks away, and that the crime rate is such and such less than in a neighborhood of comparably priced houses, etc.

At a cursory glance, a less obvious answer to "Why are the Chinese coming to Houston?" is a lack of large-scale and highly-publicized racial strife that has characterized Los Angeles, for example. Lee Kuan Yew, the former prime minister of heavily Sinicized Singapore and architect of its economic transformation spoke bluntly about American society in a 1994 interview with the journal *Foreign Affairs*: "I find parts of it totally unacceptable: guns, drugs, violent crime, vagrancy, unbecoming behaviour [sic] in public—in sum the breakdown of civil society," (as quoted in *Financial Times* 1996:18). "Houston," however, according to the same source at the Greater Houston Partnership, "has the reputation for (Chinese) immigrants of being less congested and lower in crime than the other major cities populated by Asians. The perception is that Houston is safe."

"Houston's reputation for conservative values *definitely* influences the Chinese moving here," a man highly visible in the Chinese community as a broker of a Houston Chinese real estate sales company emphasized to me in the spring of 1997. "Also, Houston is a very mobile, a very convenient city with its highway networks. It doesn't take a long time to reach great distances (although, as a veteran of Houston traffic gridlock experiences, I heard him at that point speak optimistically as a Chinese real estate *sales*man rather than simply as a Chinese man!)."

Other Chinese in the real estate profession also emphasize the educational opportunities and the school systems near the southwest Chinatown. They particularly mention Bellaire High School (which offers language courses in Chinese) and the Fort Bend school district which has a high Asian population. Further, several of my informants were not shy to offer their opinions that the education and socio-economic backgrounds of the immigrant Chinese "are among the highest levels in the Asian community here" in Houston. This often-repeated statement is striking in its comparisons and contrasts with the results of the 1996 study directed by Stephen L. Klineberg of the sociology department at Rice University who found that while the Chinese respondents in his telephone survey were more likely than other immigrants groups to mention educational opportunities as their reason for coming to Houston, almost half of the Filipinos who were contacted (whose numbers were disproportionately female in representing survey respondents) reported total household incomes of about $50,000 while 35 percent of Chinese reported incomes of the same amounts (Klineberg 1996:14). Further, 76 percent of Filipino respondents have college degrees, "but Indians and Chinese are more likely than Filipinos to have done postgraduate work," (ibid.).

A somewhat more mundane but nonetheless important attraction Houston has for Chinese was mentioned to me several times: the weather. The temperature and humidity ranges in this sprawling southeast Texas metroplex only 50 miles from the Gulf of Mexico are very similar to the quotidian environments of the other places with which they are most familiar: Taiwan, Singapore, and Hong Kong. "We couldn't take those big snow storms!" an informant laughed in early January when much of this country's eastern region was buried under record snowfalls.

The immigrants in my study also find here an already well-established Chinese community which serves the special brand of Asian communitarianism that offers social cohesion *as well as* economic dynamism. This is particularly beneficial to the extant Houston community, because Asian societies "have been able to rely on family members' Confucian sense of responsibility for each other," and "they have not needed to create tax-funded welfare states on the scale familiar in the west [sic]," (*Financial Times* 1996:18). Some Chinese in my study have pridefully said to me that they don't ask non-Chinese (i.e., the greater Houston community) for social support. Nor are they likely to patronize a non-Chinese business when the same goods or services are available within the city-wide Chinese community—no matter what the distance. For example, when the subject of food-shopping has come up in conversation, I have yet to meet someone in my study who didn't buy their basic Chinese foodstuffs at Dynasty Market on Bellaire Boulevard in Houston's southwest Chinatown. By contrast, Hong Kong Market in the same area is (deceptively) owned by a Vietnamese man (His parentage is Chinese, but within the Houston community he was always referred to me by non-Chinese as being Vietnamese.). Hong Kong Market, which is much larger than Dynasty, bristles with activity on weekends and attracts other Asians, blacks, and whites particularly to its large fresh meat and seafood counters. But none of my Chinese subjects would admit having much knowledge of the market, much less admit patronizing it (most likely because of the owner's Vietnamese identity). Further (and I find it no coincidence), when my own special relationship with the Chinese in my study group began to flower, it became obvious that there was an increased Chinese patronage of the retail supermarket business my husband and I own and operate under our last name. I know some of my informants live in the area of this business; other Chinese customers

I've seen are heretofore unfamiliar for the last 10 years we've operated this particular store in this location. The operative concept here, my husband and I agree, is *guanxi*. Although we are not Chinese, my intense interest in them and willing help with the Evergreen students' understanding and adaptation to the Western educational arena has translated into a reciprocal relationship that transcends our ethnic and cultural differences. Other businesses we own under different names (and, therefore, different identities) have not been affected by either an increase or decrease in Chinese patronage.

NOTES

1. The number of deaths from famine and battle during the Taiping Rebellion and other uprisings is recorded as a wide variance of numbers by different scholars. Lynn Pan writes that "probably sixty million people died in all," (Pan 1994:44). Jonathan D. Spence, a Western literary historian of China, writes in his masterful narrative about Hong Xiuquan that by 1864 approximately 20 million people had lost their lives in the Rebellion (Spence 1996).

2. This second and more recently developed Chinatown is described in detail on pages 11-14.

3. The Greater Houston Partnership is an organization which serves as the primary advocate for Houston's business community and is dedicated to building economic prosperity in the region. It is nearly wholly funded by private funds, with some money coming from the city and from Harris County. The Partnership is comprised of the World Trade Division, the Economic Development Division, and the Chamber of Commerce. It works closely with the mayor's office.

4. *First Colony Magazine* is a promotional tool designed to attract homeowners, business operators, and real estate investors to the First Colony development in Fort Bend County. In its public relations efforts, it included the following quotations from well-respected newspapers:
"Today's boom towns are places like Fort Bend County, Texas where the population is expected to keep growing as more people move out of Houston in

search of better schools and cheaper housing," (*The Wall Street Journal*, Tuesday, March 8, 1994).

"Population surveys place this [Fort Bend] county of nearly 300,000 people third among the nation's fastest-growing white-collar addresses, and its rapid development reflects a trend that is likely to make the state stronger, if more predictable, in years to come," (*The Washington Post*, Monday, April 4, 1994).

IV
Why a Chinese School?
And Why Evergreen?

"The doggedness with which the Chinese have hung on to their language" is a facet of Chinese identity (Pan:248). "The possession of the ancestral language is the supreme mark of being Chinese, imparting as it does a sense of unbroken continuity with the earliest years of Chinese history," (ibid.). Yet "there are some Chinese children who get no training in their heritage; they are confused about who they are," a parent told me as soon as she learned of my interest in the Houston Chinese cultural programs for children. "We call them bananas! They're white on the outside and yellow on the inside!"

This food metaphor amused me. However, I regarded very seriously the concern this mother expressed; she, like so many of the parents of Evergreen children is highly educated and has been confronted with changing venues of Chinese living their identity: most of them, like this college professor, were born on mainland China or on Chinese enclaves in Asia and fled at a young age with their parents to Taiwan when Generalissimo Chiang Kai-shek and the Nationalists lost to the communist forces of Mao Tse-tung in 1949.

The Houston Independent School District (HISD) does little to help immigrant children adjust to their new school life. Bi-lingual Spanish-English programs are taught in the lower school grades; but English as a Second Language (ESL) is the only assistance program offered in the HISD high schools. In fact, an immigrant in Houston more than three years no longer carries the alien status by the Federal and HISD standards. Only 4,000 of HISD's 203,000 students can qualify for the immigrant status, the director of special populations in the Department of Research and Evaluation told me. "And it is difficult to document these immigrants, because the information forms are filled out voluntarily by the parents," he said.

Three percent of the HISD population is Asian. Of those, the largest distributions are at the High School for Health Professions (a science magnate); Bellaire High School (a magnate school which also offers Mandarin as an elective course); and Sharpstown High School. Because there is no particular refugee status for the Chinese from pre-kindergarten through high school, a second-generation Chinese employee of HISD told me, they may benefit from ESL; but many times they fail to pass the Texas Assessment of Academic Skills (TAAS) exam. "Some students are finding it difficult to pass this English literacy exam even though they may pass English classes in school and be conditionally accepted to college."

"We have no other cultural and support programs, because of Federal funding cuts," another migrant and immigrant counselor with HISD said. "Fifty percent of my time is spent with the ESL, and the other 50 percent is spent addressing the normal problems of adolescence. I'm concerned that migrant and immigrant children (of all backgrounds) leave behind their friends and often leave behind some of their family members when they move to Houston," she continued, "but there is no official or financial way we can help them."

Nearly all of the students in my study group live in Fort Bend County and therefore are not affected by the HISD shortcomings. Nonetheless, this description of Federal and local educational programs designed to meet the needs of immigrant school-age children helps to illustrate the milieu of "reception" and "support" which confronts Chinese parents. It was their determination to create a self-referential identity—an identity the Chinese there hold for themselves in the greater world of the us-them dichotomy—that led some Chinese parents and other concerned Chinese community members to establish The Evergreen School. I will note here that the school is certainly not the first of its ilk: the modern forerunners of overseas Chinese schools were established last century in Southeast Asia as a means of reifying ethnic consciousness and social unity among the Chinese dispersed by the aforementioned episodes of upheaval during the 1800s. Also, Evergreen is just one of a growing number of Chinese language schools in Houston, all of them unrelated by administration or ownership. I queried an informant long active in Houston's Chinese community for the reason so many of these schools exist. "Quite simply, it's politics," she answered. We don't need so many schools when the attendance and size of some remains small. Many Asians (Chinese) do not feel they can achieve in the Western institutions and businesses on par with the Westerners. So, they join many different Chinese organizations to be prominent and to be able to list these accomplishments on their *résumés*. Our Chinese language schools are important to us. You know that. But the field is crowded by people who want to be able to say they've taught at one of them. I was so sick of that at the (large Chinese) school where I was the principal; I quit and went to another school where the personnel problem wasn't so bad."

Evergreen earns its highly valued reputation of excellence from the dedication of the teachers and students, the classroom attendance time (which, at three hours plus after-school Evergreen activities, exceeds other local Chinese school requirements), and the representative attendance: many of the children of civil servants in the Taiwanese government attend Evergreen (However, the Taipei Economic and Cultural Office here does not offer any particular formal endorsement of the school.).

Whereas some classrooms at Evergreen (as well as other classes at other Houston area Chinese schools) have students who speak Chinese only during the time they attend these language schools, every student in the classroom where I conducted so much of my fieldwork spoke Chinese at home as well as during their social activities. I thought it was particularly telling of their comfort in the familiar when occasionally during class some student would whisper questions or teenage "news" in Chinese while the teacher was lecturing or instructing. Certainly there were exceptional times when they spoke English. But it remained that Chinese was more often their language of choice.

Yet, it is not enough to say that Evergreen exists to teach language and culture and to make Chinese friends. As much as any other reason, the school stands as a testimony to the Chinese attitude that they remain segregated except in matters where they can benefit themselves by reaching beyond—but not allowing penetration of—their closely-knit social perimeters. That is not to say the Chinese are unfriendly to non-Chinese. Indeed, one of the Chinese journalists who was so informative about Chinese community events emphasized to me that the local Chinese want "to involve themselves in the mainstream society." Further, courteous and honorable behavior is legendary, particularly among Western accounts of social and business encounters with Chinese. But it remains that the Chinese in my study group who have been raised in the traditional manner of lifelong filial piety and honor to one's household retain an expression and self-concept of racial and cultural "purity." This is particularly obvious in the remarks parents made to me regarding dating circumstances of their older children. One such instance occurred when an older woman whose youngest son (a former Evergreen student now living in another city) commented on her son's roommate.

"He's so much like Buddy. He and Buddy think alike and get along well. But the roommate will only date girls with red hair."

"Really?! And he's Chinese?"

"No, he's American."

"But Buddy is American," I quickly responded, knowing Buddy was born in the States and without thinking that his parents were born in China.

There followed a few moments of silence. I could have kicked myself.

"Oh, you mean the roommate is of European origin," I offered, feebly.

"Yes," she replied.

It is incorrect to assume that everyone involved with Evergreen is a parent or a professional teacher. I met several Chinese, including Jack, the man who taught the class where I spent so much of my time, who had no children or relatives that attended or administered the school. I wondered why these people were taking their weekends to be there when they could be with their spouses or friends or playing golf or some other such activity.

"Well," he answered as humbly as the word spoken in three syllables would allow, "I feel I've gotten so much from the community, and I think it's time to give something back."

"Which community?" I thought to myself, although I had to believe he meant the Houston Chinese community. As he continued, my suspicions were confirmed.

"I came to this country with a (college) degree but I didn't know anyone except the people who hired me in Taiwan and brought me here. I didn't even know much English. I've stayed here for almost twelve years. I miss my family in Taiwan a lot. But I'm an adult, and I've had to adjust. I've always felt I still had some connection to home, because here (in southwest Chinatown where he was speaking to me) I could go to any number of places and pick up several newspapers that would keep me informed about events in Chinese. I've also met a lot of people through Chinese community events, through Chinese businesses where I shop and spend time, and through friends. It's time I gave back to the community. Besides, when I have children, I want them to learn Chinese and have Chinese friends, too. I'll probably be living here for awhile."

Was his desire to have children who would have Chinese friends and probably attend the Evergreen school going to enhance (even in his small, individual contribution) a social division between the Chinese and everyone else? Does he intend to live as a Chinese in Houston or as a Chinese-American (He became a U. S. citizen two years ago.)? As a teacher at Evergreen wasn't he a figure of authority who could and did influence the identity formation/perpetuation of these kids? There is so much in the rhetoric of this physical classroom arrangement and in his actions there that supports as well as contradicts the messages these kids are getting. And in some cases, what is left unsaid and undone is as much a rhetorical message.

Because the Evergreen facilities are leased from the Jesuit school where the academic props and religious messages *in situ* during the week remain on the weekend, the Chinese students operate within an environment created for them by people who are (with only a few exceptions) from a different ethnic (and largely otherwise religious and philosophical) group. In this lease agreement, the Chinese use nearly every campus facility on the weekends, from the basketball court in the gymnasium to the cafeteria where calligraphy classes are held, to the outdoor fields where the students play volleyball and hold carnivals to raise money for Evergreen.

My first impression remains the strongest: the spacious classroom where Jack teaches and where I did so much of my fieldwork is the same class the Jesuits use to teach world history. And, ironically, the door to this classroom locks automatically so as to admit no one from the outside once the students are in; it is at the benevolence of whoever sees the outsider trying to enter that he or she is approached from inside the classroom, the doorknob turned, and the person allowed in! Of course, during the time I spent in that classroom, the Chinese and I were the only ones there. But it remained that we were *zhonghua,* and the Others on the periphery had to pay a tributary "thank you" for our recognizing them and allowing them to be among us.[1]

Just to the inside of the classroom door nailed to the wall is a crucifix which appears to be about a foot long and eight inches wide. Christ hangs his head toward anyone passing through the door. He's dark-haired, and his skin tone is a most unusual color that I could never identify as belonging exclusively to any particular ethnic group: depending upon the attitude of the viewer, He could be European, Indian, African, Australian, or—yes,—Asian.

Thirty chairs are attached to full-size desks (as contrasted with the old-style university half-desk that is actually a right or left-handed extension of the arm), and they are arranged in a horseshoe shape three and four rows deep facing the largest of the chalkboards and the tall metal stool on which Jack usually sits when reading to the class or calling upon each student to respond in Chinese. These molded plastic chairs, like the other facilities at the school, appear to be new or at least to be well-maintained. Under each of them is a metal rack for storing books and students' classroom materials. The students in my class always sat at these desks with attentive posture or leaned over their work when they focused on reading or writing; they never folded their arms across their chests as a sign of resentment or disagreement. Occasionally there was a relaxed posture, particularly of the girls, of turning sideways in their chairs and putting their feet on the book rack under their neighbor's chair; and some of the taller, lankier boys assumed an extended-leg slouch downwards in their chairs while listening to Jack speak, but this was not the kind of body language that said someone was disinterested or disrespectful. All of this contrasted each time there was a ten-minute break period: invariably, ABC (American-born Chinese) students from lower-competency classrooms would come into our classroom and want to socialize with our group; they were always louder and physically intrusive, sitting on the desks to talk to the Chinese in my class, leaning over them to see how more advanced this class's material compared to their own, talking and laughing out loud about their peers. There is quite a bit of open floor space in the room that accommodates—even encourages—loitering. When the break-time visitors were gone, this open space with its white floor tiles was a strong focal area for Jack to walk about passing chalk back and forth between his hands while engaging the students in a pleasing manner to respond to his questions. The atmosphere was always friendly and fairly relaxed; the only pressure to perform seemed to come from the students who each appeared quite concerned to respond correctly. As Pye explains, the rigid achievement structure of Confucian culture is in place in China but is able to blossom and become even more successful in the more open atmosphere of, say, American society, "while at home the demands of conformity stifle their innovative and achievement drives," (Pye 1985:289-290). Said another way, the standards of conformity and achievement remain high among my study group of Chinese; and although respect for authority and responsibility to achieve the parents' goals remains elevated, the path to those goals is not as predatory and competitive in Houston as it would be in Taiwan or other locales where the Chinese are the dominant group.

There are two maps in the room, one of which is a cartographic representation of the world, with North and South America centered on this framed, inflexible plastic form that is molded to indicate elevations; and the other is the type often-used to show larger portions by printing various areas on large sheets of paper (about three feet in height by four feet in width), hinging them horizontally at the top, and placing this "flip pad" on a stand so that a particular map can be flipped to in the stack and displayed. The flip-style map remained turned to Europe in all my time at Evergreen except, ironically, that last day of formal fieldwork in the classroom; on that day, for some still inexplicable reason, the map was turned to illustrate how the United States was cartographically represented during the period 1820-1850: the period inclusive of the Opium War and the beginning of the great waves of Chinese migration! Further, the map was titled, "Our America: Backgrounds and Development"!

Whenever Jack referred to a physical area of China, he either located the place on the smaller plastic map with elevations (and a large black hole where the western edge of the Caucuses Mountains should have been but was removed from the face of the world [map] by some unexplained event; once again ironically, since the derivative word "Caucasian" was inapplicable to their concern with Chinese education, culture, and identity); or he usually handed out small mimeographed maps of mainland China which included the South China Sea and the island of Taiwan. These small maps included without explanation the entire geographical area of Tibet invaded by Mao's forces and stolen from the Tibetan people. At first, I gently pointed out to Jack and the students within earshot that indeed China had appropriated this pristine region and renamed it as their own. The response to me was not unlike the eyes of a deer spotted by the headlamps of the oncoming car: a look which is indistinctive of surprise and ignorance. I couldn't help but think that this political experience was beyond the "village mentality" of concern with one's own or was inapplicable to the Chinese sense of networking. (I'll remind the reader of the ancient Chinese saying I included earlier, "*Tian gao huangdi yuan.*").[2] In deference to the teacher and the educational agenda he wanted to cover, as well in deference to the students who had no need of an outsider telling them at that time what I wish they knew, I let this initial lack of response to geographical impropriety pass quietly. In the following pages, you will read that I took up the issue again, quietly, when the opportunity rose. I also gave to an adult informant a book written by a Western observer of the atrocities Tibetans are suffering at the administrative hands of the communist Chinese; the book I chose, *In Exile Beyond the Land of the Snows,* is well-acclaimed, and the copy I gave her is translated into Chinese and signed by the author, John Avedon.

Chinese parents often expressed to me their concern that their children retain their language and traditional attitudes and behavior of respecting authority and having good *li*. Pye tells us that historically "the three most striking characteristics of the Chinese family were the paramount value of filial piety, the absolute denial of the legitimacy of all forms of aggression, and the vision of a rigidly defined order of role relationships. These three characteristics were closely interrelated and of critical importance in shaping the personality, " (Pye 1992:91). He adds that "no other culture in history has placed such a stress upon filial piety as had the Chinese. Traditional Chinese literature and philosophy constantly held up as the ultimate virtue the spirit of dutiful respect for parents. In recording their history the Chinese developed as cultural heroes the individuals who excelled in this particular virtue. Thus the dynastic histories recorded the lives not only of great officials, conquering soldiers, and distinguished scholars but also those of exemplary filial sons and daughters," (ibid.:91-92). With this in mind, I asked the students to tell me why they took their weekends to attend Chinese school. Did their parents give them an option? Were they angry that much of their "free" time had to be devoted to not only studying but also to excelling in yet another subject?

Since China scholars tell us that the young Chinese child is expected to see no faults in his parents and to dismiss any shortcomings in the parents that he sees as he grows older, "he can never speak about them and certainly he can never act against them. Traditionally the child was taught to separate emotion from action, and his capacity for feeling, shouting, and above all, acting against adult power was eliminated. To be able to live with strict and inhibiting norms was in the Confucian view the path to omnipotence," which later was interpreted as meaning that omnipotence came merely from having suffered at the hand of the older generations and the greater powers, (Pye 1992:76). It wasn't surprising, therefore, that "My parents make me come," was the response of many students to me. Moreover, throughout millennia of Chinese civilization respecting authority was exacted at the price of alternatively being shamed. Indeed, Pye tells us, a child who makes mistakes or refuses to acknowledge the authority of his parents will be disciplined in the home, often in "a ruthless use of shame. The child is made to feel the humiliation of his errors and to believe that whenever he fails in meeting the appropriate standards of behavior others will look down on him," (Pye 1992:95). This Chinese concept of saving and losing "face" (*zhichi*) is often addressed by anthropologists, and a distinction is made between shame and guilt (Hu 1944:45-64; Hsu 1953. Pye makes these references to both Hu and Hsu in Pye 1992:96.). Further, Chinese have been exemplified for having a "shame" culture, but I believe this distinction lacks much merit. Surely, fear of humiliation could be a motivating factor in the students' diligent study habits and ambition to achieve high academic honors; moreover, self-discipline had its obvious rewards for this older group of students in my class (one-fourth of whom were graduating from high school as I finished my fieldwork, and all of them were applying to universities which required elite academic achievement). But what about the dynamics of this in the daily socialization process? Were the students repressing an anger that could be the natural outcome of the aggression they might feel from being forced by their parents and Chinese teachers to do some things while being denied the opportunity to do others?

I took the opportunity of there being another substitute teacher one day (not the same friend who originally invited me to Chinese school with her) to ask her why she thought the students were taking their time to be at Evergreen on the weekends and study Chinese during the schoolweek. This woman, also an Evergreen parent, fit the educational and language profile of the other parents I had met; so I expected her response to coincide with that of the students. "Ask them," she said, "and they'll tell you that they come because their friends are here."

"I *did* ask them," I emphasized, "and they told me that they come because their parents make them come."

This lady then laughed nervously, and I believe she was embarrassed that I (an Other) gave the more realistic answer to my own question. For me, it was an interesting brief encounter. She conducted the class rather formally (certainly moreso than Jack ever attempted) and with far less humor than any of us were accustomed to in the classroom's normal atmosphere. Everyone in the room sat a bit more straight that day, refrained from informal chit-chat except during break time, and didn't linger when the final bell of the afternoon rang.

"Of course they would rather be doing something else," a former principal of the school told me. "Few of these kids go willingly. But they have to obey their parents. That's our way. We expect them to do what we tell them they must do. You'll be surprised how many of them will complain about being at Evergreen now; but when they get to college they take classes in Chinese history, literature, and language. They'll have Chinese friends, too."

Her prediction was based on her personal experience as well as her observations at the college where she teaches. One of her two older daughters was rebellious during her high school dating years and refused to date Chinese boys. But later, the mother told me with a sigh of relief, she gradually began dating Asian boys and finally found a Chinese boyfriend with whom she is engaged. The daughter told her a few months ago that she is more comfortable in that relationship, because of the commonalties the two share.

NOTES

1. On page 22 I employed *zhonghua* as the Chinese term which describes the attitude of the Chinese as belonging to a country which is culturally centered and implies that the peripheral countries surrounding China were populated by culturally inferior barbarians.

2. *Tian gao huangdi yuan* expressed a feeling of village people that imperial intervention in their local society was remote. I use this phrase on page 19.

Hermeneutics

V

The Other: Informant or Anthropologist?

From the very beginning of my fieldwork, I was keenly aware that the Other existed in the relationship of the Chinese and the anthropologist. What I found subject to interpretation is just who the "Other" is in the relationship/opposition of identity and difference. Other than their racial features and what I considered to be their exceedingly polite manner around non-Chinese, was there really anything *different* about the Chinese? Did they have different ideas about their personal conduct? By being in this country, did they aspire to many of the same things as Westerners of the same economic and educational status? Did they frequent the same restaurants, the same supermarkets, the same entertainment and recreational activities? Why weren't there many of *them* in *my* world throughout the day? And how would all this, and more, affect the lines of communication between the two disparate groups?

Deborah Tannen addresses the issues of difference and dominance within a framework of interpreting discourse in her monograph, *Gender and Discourse* (1994). Her consideration is whether the two phenomena of cultural difference and power can be conceptualized as mutually exclusive poles within theoretical literary approaches which often place gender and language into either of the two categories: "the 'cultural difference' approach, as opposed to a 'power' or 'dominance' approach," (Tannen 1994:9). Citing the work of linguistic scholars (including her own work) in this and related fields, she is compelled "to confront and counteract the social inequality that results from negative stereotyping of minority cultural groups," (ibid.). Her concern is that relations between a member of a dominant group and a member of a subjected group are affected by misunderstandings of such things as differences in conventional ways of showing listenership or differences in conversational styles. Tannen's comments on this gender/power dichotomy are appropriate when applied to anthropologists, because it is we who must be made accountable to those we study. Moreover, they are important considerations in distinguishing identity (sameness) from difference (that which carries apart meaning from sameness). This, of course, is an irretractable consideration when judging their comments on such issues as race, social pathologies, and family obligations.

Tyler tells us in *The Unspeakable* (1987) that "it is one of the paradoxes of Western thought, and the essential problem of our time, that this world of abstraction can represent only by destroying what it seeks to represent, and though it may seem odd, if not perverse, to think of writing a grammar or an ethnography as an act of violence, that is how these seemingly humane, scholarly ethnographies have been 'expropriated' (Said 1978). Though we may deny colonial intent, there is a clear parallel here between Plato and the poets, and the anthropologist and his people, for just as Plato took from his Republic, so too does the anthropologist and the linguist take inspiration from his people while denying them any place in the kingdom of his text. It may be, as Nietzsche claimed, that all representation is violent, but it seems more reasonable to suspect the modes and purposes of representation rather than representation itself, for it is these elements of the rhetorical context which the text must obscure or falsify in order to be a text," (Tyler 1987:65).

In the course of my fieldwork, I enjoyed a relationship with the students that was always friendly and animated but also marked by polite separation. Clearly, anyone different (the anthropologist) changes the equation by her presence there. Distinctive markers between them (collectively) and me (individually) were mostly demonstrative of power/authority: I was as old as their teacher and about the same age as some of their parents; and I was a student at Rice University, a school their parents held up to them as epitomizing educational excellence. But more cogently was the status of my race and *raison d'être* at Evergreen. Undeniably, being white in America is still a marker of elitism. Whites remain the socially, economically, and culturally dominant group. Further, my being an older white woman in some ways for them was representative of the economic power that the students' parents worked very hard to profit from. So, my being there as a graduate student interested in them gave me a particular status that was enhanced by the teacher's encouragement that they talk to me about themselves.

Tannen writes that the consequences of style differences work to the disadvantage of members of minority groups, which are stigmatized in our society, while working to the advantage of those who have the power to enforce their interpretations. "Socially determined power differences are an inextricable element of cultural difference theory and research," she points out (Tannen:8). Further, she says, the Observer has no clear means of interpreting—much less, representing—the Observed if all the former does is to examine the latter from a separate (i.e. removed, different) position. Citing the neurologist and essayist Oliver Sacks, she says he "demonstrates that in order to understand a medical condition, physicians need to not only examine their patients but also listen to them. Whereas modern medicine may provide invaluable insight into chemical and biological courses of disease, only patients hold the clues to what their diseases are 'really like'. . .In the same spirit, attention to how participants experience conversations under analysis provides invaluable insight into the workings of interaction that are otherwise unavailable to the researcher," (ibid.:6).

Further, what Tyler writes of linguistic analysis and expression in *The Said and the Unsaid* (1978) is applicable to encountering and attempting to understand the Other through an otherwise solipsistic Cartesian *cogito* ego if we can "be said to have knowledge of or be conscious of a system of meanings, private or public, other than those of verbal thought," (Tyler 1978:82). He reminds us that some acquired skills become habitual, being performed without conscious guidance and verbal direction, "becoming so assimilated as to be autonomous, involuntary, and unverbalizable," (ibid.:83).

"At a minimum, then, the ego is aware of its own body, is conscious of it in a way that is not simply verbal, is aware of it in this way even when thinking verbally, and is aware of the fact that neither verbal thought nor consciousness of the body fully constitutes descriptions of the body or directs and orchestrates its movement and operation. The source of our sense of self then is less in the fact that we think thoughts than in the fact that we are aware of inhabiting bodies that dispose themselves toward their own components and the world without our say so (Merlau-Ponty 1964:93). The self arises then not from any consciousness of thinking and of being the master of thoughts but from an awareness of its limitations, of there being things within its own domain of which it may be the object rather than the agent. This internal consequence of the awareness of the 'otherness' of the body parallels the ego's awareness of others in the external world, its awareness that others can turn about or reciprocate its sense of agency and make it an object of their agency much as the body does," (Tyler 1978:83)

It was only by acknowledging the consequences of style differences and the habitual non-verbal means of expression and awareness of Otherness that I could undertake my fieldwork with these students, because it is considered that "throughout the world there has been a tendency to look upon the Chinese as a closed group without serious internal divisions," (Chen and von der Mehden:6). And to the extent that their deliberate ethnic segregation, their propensity for forming exclusive communities on the basis of their Old World heritage of kinship systems and personal relations is instrumental to that effect, non-Chinese have been able to surmise that little could affect Chinese racial pride and intransigence (cf. Siu:4). This foundation of Chinese society was poignantly illustrated one afternoon in class at the beginning of my second year of fieldwork when I was unexpectedly called upon by the Evergreen teacher to talk to the students about how to avoid racism.

"You're the expert in this, " he said.

I was surprised at his distinguishing me this way in front of the students; but in that nano-second in which one has to make a decision, I thought that if I were to protest that distinction or try to defer my comments from the subject I would be: 1) injuring in his eyes and the students' eyes my credibility as an anthropologist who studies cultural expressions of a people's beliefs and practices and hence (possibly in their eyes) must be an authority on the possible clashes which arise between groups that misunderstand each other or harbor anger and hatred toward the other; and 2) I would be speaking to a young audience (from grades seventh through high school) of wide-ranging personal/social experiences, and how *they* thought I talked to them (e.g., as an adult their parents' age, or as a like-student, or as an expert in the field of human relations), would greatly affect from their position how I might be able to interact in the future with them as informants.

The resolution of that nano-second? I told them to continue their language and cultural studies which gave them a sense of self-constructed ownership of themselves as well as gave them a sense of being worthy inheritors of their distinctive cultural history. At that point I told them that one of the things I feel so sad about in this age of mass connectedness is the demise of so many languages which succumb to the wider use of the more dominant languages of commerce and politics, because their loss means the loss of different perspectives the world so greatly needs.

"I applaud you for raising your Chinese literacy," I said. "It gives you an additional perspective on the world which you can use to create understanding about yourself for others who know nothing about you and may otherwise fabricate malicious attitudes toward you. Further, my advice is to learn to appreciate differences and always treat others as you would like to be treated."

Throughout the brief time I spoke, I wondered about the impression I was making on them. I must have played well to what they wanted to hear, because several of the students applauded when I finished.

After a break was called, I asked Jack, the classroom teacher, about what compelled him to have me talk about racism.

"Well, the other night I was watching *48 Hours* on television, and Dan Rather began the program with a warning that the evening's agenda would deal with racism and that in the film footage and discourse some of the language would be offensive to some viewers. I thought, 'Why do the words have to be repeated if the producers know that some people will be offended, even hurt?' I am amazed at the number of times I'm invited to someone's home for socializing with a group where someone will begin to say something derogatory about another ethnic group; the speaker seems oblivious to whether there are others in the room who don't share his or her sentiments. And so often no one offers an objection to the speaker. It seems to me that a younger group of Chinese do not hold the racist attitudes and practices that their parents do. The younger Chinese are more tolerant. They're attending desegregated schools whereas their parents not only attended segregated schools but also practice discrimination in their hiring practices at work and in the kind of businesses they patronize."

His attitude that these kids "do not hold racist attitudes and practices that their parents do" was rather naive, I first thought (cf. Chang:52). I wondered how he could expect adolescents—especially those raised in the strict, time-honored tradition of filial piety, *not* to absorb the attitudes of their parents?! Their non-questioning of the authority of their parents' attitudes was indicative of the succession and continuity of the Chinese way. And, hence, this was a contributing factor to identity formation of these newest Chinese immigrants. Yet, I came to steadfastly believe that the verbal expressions of "racism" were more their reaction to a perceived threat to their cultural purity and philosophical harmony than a testimony of hatred and intended harm to a non-Chinese group.

Only a few class periods before that day, three girls (two from the eighth grade and one a freshman in high school) who were visiting the classroom from a less advanced class at Evergreen, and who were thus exempt from the class exam being administered, eagerly gathered around me to talk. It was obvious to them that I was an anomaly to the class of ethnic Chinese! They asked me why I was there, and when I explained I was doing research on Chinese identity they eagerly began talking to me. In fact, their enthusiasm to give me their opinions was far above moderated tones, and we had to go outside the building to some benches in a garden area. Relaxed, they blurted these statements:

"In my middle school (which had quite a number of Asian students, she said) we pretty much mix with the other groups."

"Yeah, but it's not like that in high school," the older one said. "All the Asians stick together in cliquish groups. It's pretty obvious that the whites and Mexicans don't like us too much. They call us names and make fun of the way we look."

"Do you have any white friends?" I asked.

"Oh, yeah, my parents think that's okay if they come from nice homes. But they would rather that I have Chinese friends," an eighth-grader replied.

"What kind of work do your parents do? Are they with non-Chinese during the day?" I inquired.

One girl's father worked for the communications department of the Taipei Economic and Cultural Office in Houston. Of the other two, one owned a local produce company; and the mother of the second girl worked in this same business. The scion of the owner of the produce company replied:

"My parents won't hire any blacks or Mexicans. They don't like the Vietnamese, either."

"Why not?" I asked.

"Because they (the parents) say they can't trust them (particularly the blacks and Mexicans, and the Vietnamese to a lesser extent). (I came to understand that "Mexicans" meant anyone from Latin America.) My parents say that the blacks and Mexicans are not dependable and that they don't work hard."

"Working hard" was a theme repeated in conversations with Chinese youth and adults alike. Never did I hear something like "working smart;" rather, "working hard" was a metaphor for an unadulterated dedication to an assigned task or was a display of duty which would not be interrupted until all effort toward honoring that duty was seemingly exhausted. Time was a big factor in this equation: if one spent long uninterrupted hours—often in solitary pursuit—of a project, then one is said to have worked hard. Also, "pleasure" was never associated with working hard; pleasure wasn't serious enough. "Duty" was the far more appropriate association with working hard.

I continued my query about their parents' attitudes toward other people. "And the Vietnamese?" was my next direction of curiosity.

"They just don't feel about them like they do the Chinese. They will hire white people, though."

What did they think of me? As the reader will see in another section, I was invited to sponsor an after-school program for the Evergreen kids; clearly, from the invitation, I had some place of authority or leadership for them, or at least I can say I was liked. I never wanted to create an uncomfortable formal atmosphere by asking them, "What do you think about my being here, watching you, and asking you all these questions?" But I know by the way some of the kids approached me and volunteered information about themselves that they wanted me to know about them, that they felt comfortable with my presence and with their sharing this information. I also knew that I was being watched, and how closely I was watched surprised me: one day I lost one of five distinctive tribal bangle bracelets I had been given in Kenya; I searched the room and even retraced my steps outside around the campus and into the gymnasium. The youngest student in the room *behind* whom I happened to be sitting that afternoon turned around after I returned from my fruitless search and asked if I had found the bracelet. "No," I answered sadly, because the bracelets had a sentimental quality for me. "You were wearing only four earlier today," he responded! And while I thought he was showing me sympathy and possibly encouragement that I really didn't lose one of these narrow little bracelets at all, I was astonished that this young boy, *sitting in front of me*, even noticed such minute details about me! Another time, I attended a Chinese production of King Lear in which Jack played the title role and some of the students from my Evergreen class played various roles of importance, including one young lady who played Fool. The production qualities were first rate for this local Chinese amateur theater group. Smoke billowed and lights flashed when Lear went mad; lines were enunciated clearly and effectively; and beautiful costumes spoke to the strength of the Zhou dynastic period. My family and I stayed throughout the nighttime presentation at Miller Outdoor Theatre in one of Houston's largest and most popular parks, and we saw a number of my other classmates during intermissions. But alas, the late nighttime and cool air took a soporific toll on my young daughter, so we left during the final battle scene. The next day in class, I was so surprised that Jack numerous times asked me where I was sitting the night before. "I kept looking for you," he repeated; and I felt compelled to convince him by describing not only the scenes I thought he excelled in but also by detailing row and seats where we sat!

There were other similar incidents of them watching me when I least suspected it. At this time, I'm still trying to sort out for my own understanding just where I was placed in their lives. One thing remains certain: I can only accomplish this understanding by separating the same and the different.

VI

Philosophical Thought and Religion

It is without a doubt that the structure of Confucianism with its emphasis on kinship, community, authority, and right moral order has the oldest and most profound impact on one's modeling one's self as Chinese. There are some scholars who view 20th century China from the perspective of the country emerging from millennia of political and cultural isolation, its sensibilities assaulted by the encounter with alternative claims to civilizations which could rival the physical, ideological, and institutional strength of China (i.e., the Opium War of the 19th century) (cf. Dirlik 1991 and 1978). "Such a change of consciousness accompanied the articulation of a nationalist political ideology in China at the turn of the century," writes Arif Dirlik from his viewpoint of the Chinese reconceptualizing their political space in an expression of nationalism and revolution (Dirlik 1991:51). "If we perceive nationalism in terms of its global revolutionary premises rather than its parochial manifestations, it is not surprising that the first Chinese to raise the question of China's reorganization as a nation were not the conservative defenders of the Confucian political order, who continued to insist that China was a world unto itself and that the Chinese world contained all the necessary institutions for a civilized world. They were those Chinese who, having discovered other societies with their own institutions, were willing to recognize alternative claims to civilization—and even that those claims were more suitable to the age than the claims to the Confucian political order, which has been designed for circumstances when China's civilization had no competitors," (ibid.) This is said to have led to a "radical reinterpretation of Chinese history made possible by the introduction of Marxist historical theory to China after 1919," (Dirlik 1978:2). "The radical break of Marxist historians with their predecessors becomes evident when their conceptualization of Chinese history is contrasted to the inherited view of history represented by the Confucian historical tradition," Dirlik writes (ibid:7). "The Marxist outlook on Chinese history inverted the traditional Confucian view of the past," (ibid). However, the Chinese in my study value the pre-Marxist cultural heritage of their ancestors, and they have transported it and have accommodated it to their present life in Houston. It was, therefore, to my great surprise that early January to mid-October passed in my Evergreen classroom without the slightest mention of Confucius or his teachings.

I telephoned Jack one morning at his office and asked him about his Confucian training in Taiwan (at school as well as at home) and why he seemingly had not felt compelled to teach the same at Evergreen. The results of that conversation, as well as other conversations I had on this topic with other informants, will follow after we concern ourselves with a background of Chinese philosophy and religion.

As early as the Shang dynasty (1766-1122 B.C.) we have evidence on the recorded inscriptions of oracle bones that gods and ancestral deities were addressed in the concepts of reverence, filiality, kingly virtue, propriety in the performance of ritual, etc. (de Bary 1988:1). Also, Buddhism and Religious Daoism, as well as Christianity to some extent, have had significant influences on the lives of the Chinese. Indeed, in Smith's words, "The most striking feature of traditional Chinese thought as a whole is its extraordinary eclecticism, its ability to tolerate diverse and sometimes seemingly incompatible notions with little sense of conflict or contradiction. In part, this remarkable integrative capacity can be explained by the powerful Chinese impulse to find unity in all realms of experience, human and supernatural," (Smith:129).

One might be tempted to think that all religious practices must have shared a common denominator in order to have made inroads to the patterned thinking and practices of a country which remained mostly isolated for nearly all of the archaeological record until just the last century. In its state of high conceit and physical isolation, its philosophical thought and religious practices remained largely cohesive and consistent while its borders remained largely impenetrable (cf. Smith:137-138). It remains for us to examine, briefly, what distinguished the deviant practices (*not* in the sense of perversion, but rather in the sense of existing apart from the dominant philosophical standards) and how the Chinese have accommodated them alongside the traditional influence of Confucianism which many will agree continued to exist as a "ghost" even during the time of discreditation and later appropriation by the communists in the People's Republic of China (cf. *The Economist*).

Smith's identification of Chinese thought (and—implied—beliefs) as eclectic is further understood by Rose Hum Lee's description that the average Chinese is an ethical eclectic as well as a religious eclectic. She writes that one of the paradoxes in considering Chinese beliefs is to differentiate between ethical and religious origins; because rather than choose between the two ethical systems of Confucianism and Daoism and choose between two religious systems (specifically, Buddhism and Daoism), "the average Chinese selects from each what is meaningful to him. The final mixture is illogical and confusing to westerners [sic], but rewarding to the polytheistic Chinese," (Lee 1960:278-279).

Although Lee wrote these words more than 35 years ago, she could have drawn the same conclusions from many of my informants. I found among the students as well as among some of the adults that they attended church at two of the larger Chinese Christian churches in town (often traveling more than 20 miles round trip to do so) as well as visited the Chinese Jade Buddha Temple at times which they considered propitious for the memory of their ancestors. None of these Chinese I spoke with saw anything contradictory in that. Rather, the question I had about their "supporting" both places was shrugged off with comments like, "I see no problem." The Christian church experience seemed attractive to them for the fellowship of the very active youth group, and the Buddhist experience satisfied an obligation of reverence to their departed family members.

"You should see a Chinese funeral," a Chinese Christian (Protestant) university junior encouraged me. "You'll be amazed to see the mixed symbols and meanings. For example, there's sometimes a

Buddhist carrying a cross. And when the service is over, the body is cremated. We don't think this is unusual even though we are dedicated to our religion."

She continued to offer explanations of other examples of a Chinese brand of Christianity which departs from the mainstream Western source: "We recognize Christmas as the birth of Jesus, but we don't celebrate it with any gifts under the tree nor a visit from Santa Claus. We get red envelopes with money inside. That's the same means of gift-giving at Chinese New Year."

Another university student in Houston from a different part of the United States added that his family also had strong ties to Christianity (although these ties were not so binding on him); and he supported the expression of this first students' comments on Chinese religious eclecticism. "The Chinese Christian church (Protestant) practices are very mixed," he said, while adding that his family remains dedicated to the religion.

Lee further offers that an "explanation to this is best sought in the understanding of kinship systems which early in China's history revolved around the clan; the two ethical systems of Confucianism and Daoism were appropriated by the clan to establish inter-clan and intra-clan relationships and to formalize them with ritualistic observances. "Hence," Lee tells us, "familial relationships became interwoven with the two ethical systems, the Confucian dominating. Because clans ruled China, by the founding of dynasties, the ethical systems became interlaced with familial and political institutions," (ibid.:278).

Both Confucianism and Daoism originated in the sixth century B.C., and while the former advocated a return to the lost virtues of the early Zhou dynasty (1122-256 B.C.)—to family-centered ethics, ritual, and social responsibility—the Daoists "sought release from social burdens; they were at heart individualists and escapists, concerned less with changing the world in an active way than with finding their special niche in the natural order," (Smith:30). This is not the primary explanation for grounding philosophy and religion in China, however. Antecedent to these two ethical systems was the profound Chinese view of the universe as a naturally-unified harmonious cosmic whole, self-contained, self-operating, spontaneously generated and perpetually in motion. The cooperative and synchronically interacting universe proceeded from a pattern or process which mandated that all things follow the internal dictates of their own natures and thus required no creator (ibid.:130). It follows that by "lacking the idea of a personalistic creator external to the cosmos, the Chinese developed an approach to religious life that led them to reject both monotheism and theological absolutism;" of course, this "weakened the prospects for institutional religion and kept China from developing a concept of evil as an active force in the personified Western sense," because the goal of Confucianism was social harmony rather than personal salvation (ibid.:133). Self-realization could never be removed from one's duty of service to humanity. Neither the introductions of the kinship-renouncing doctrine of Buddhism; nor the later neo-Confucian metaphysics which promulgated the idea of a Supreme Ultimate (*taiji*) and also served as the source of principles (*li*) around which material force coalesced to comprise all things; nor the saving grace of Christianity did anything to alter these basic features of Chinese religious life (ibid.:134; cf. Ambrose). To do so would disturb the relation forces classified by the cosmic terms *yin* and *yang* which were always relative concepts rather than unyielding categories.

Because Confucian social theory is concerned with the harmonious workings of the universe, one must find his place(s) within the system in variance with the different *guanxi*. This defines someone as social or interactive, never as an isolated or separate being. Ambrose tells us that the Chinese character for benevolence means "two men." "Indeed, there is no concept of man as separate from men," (Ambrose:65). So we come to understand that what constitutes proper human relationships is the central emphasis of Confucianism: that one is seen in relation to someone else is not just a means of identity; it is the standard of Chinese culture and society.

"Someone is born *into* the Confucist system; Confucianism is set for them," an informant from the mainland told me. But "no one calls himself a Confucist" (as one would call himself a Christian or a Buddhist).

This same informant reminded me of the Confucian emphasis on scholarship and learning which some believe had no parallel in Western culture (cf. *Financial Times*). Imagine, then, my surprise that after spending so much time in the classroom Jack still had not raised these principles in any form of direct pedagogy or referential stories of "right behavior." My major concern when I telephoned him was that by raising this issue (of what I admit I thought was his being remiss) he would be embarrassed. Jack, after all, was born in Taiwan to Han Chinese parents. And not only did I remain fully aware during my fieldwork that I was a white woman among Chinese, but my obvious knowledge of Chinese history and comprehension of cultural difference visibly amazed this man and compelled him on numerous occasions to verify a date I assigned a dynasty or translate a Chinese term into English. Fortunately, for my sense of "face," I was always right. But the answers I gave to questions he could not easily answer *a cappella* were always offered with some (quiet) trepidation on my part. I simply didn't want this man to appear less sophisticated to himself nor in front of his students. Nonetheless, while this remained a delicate operation on my part, Jack continued (to my relief) to call on me as an "expert."

He responded to my question about teaching Confucianism in the classroom (and I think I rightly interpreted his voice to sound a little sheepish) that the woman who taught the same group prior to his coming to Evergreen had used a Confucian text that was intended for middle school-age students. "I think it's important to teach the kids moral standards; but when I started talking about moral standards and Confucius' sayings, the kids got bored. I would prefer to teach *Lunyu* (the work known as *Analects*, one of the "Four Books," or *sishu*, of Confucian teaching)," he continued.

When I asked him whether he taught the philosophical teachings of Mencius who said "man is basically good" or whether he also covered other Confucian interpretations, he replied that he found that the kids were more receptive to Laozi teachings, "because Laozi taught that the world is predetermined by heaven and the gods," Jack said. "'Don't do anything against nature'," he attributed to the sixth century B.C. philosopher who predated Confucius.

"But isn't that Daoism?" I asked.

Jack was non-committal in his response. Instead, he said that rather than teach Confucius' sayings by using a textbook, the kids might be more receptive to his telling a story, to using examples of how to live.

I encouraged Jack not to put off teaching Confucius just because the kids said they were bored. "They're adolescents," I pointed out to him (Jack has no children and no previous teaching experience.). "They're just pushing you to see how far they can get without having to memorize or at least study Confucius. They know that if they were still in Taiwan, they would have to study him during the school year just as you did when you were growing up." (Other informants not too much older than Jack had told me that during their school years in Taiwan they had entire courses devoted to Confucius during their middle school and high school years.)

"Well, maybe you're right," he replied.

I was very amused—and pleased for the kids and for Jack—when the following Sunday Jack handed out Confucian text books and spent the entire afternoon study time acting out and translating Confucius! When I told him I was happy to see he had reconsidered, he said, "Well, these are high school texts that a father of one of the students gave me. The other texts were for middle school. The kids seem to be more interested now."

Some weeks later, I brought the subject of Confucianism up informally among some students in the Evergreen classroom when Jack was not present. Rather than respond with an audible groan that they might have to study the sage again in class, they appeared prepared, even comfortable at the prospect that they would have formalized for them what I perceived was being taught (or at least practiced) in their homes. After all, authoritarianism is a legacy of Confucian thought which saw the relationship between highers and lowers not unlike the relationship between a master and a pupil: the people's welfare was a central principle of Confucianism, and the ruler was expected to instruct and mold them. Although I did not reveal this to my informants, my suspicions increased that what I was seeing in Jack was a man wanting to help instruct younger Chinese but uncertain about taking the responsibility to mold them along traditional lines. His lack of family ties to this area (although he has a sister, brother-in-law, and nieces and nephews only 30 miles away) and his childless marriage to an immigrant Hong Kong woman, as well as his employment as the only Chinese and only man in his department at a Western company, seems to be circumstantial chaff which separates him from the kernel of his heritage. I began to see him somewhat as an anomaly, uncertain of his position in the community and trying more than any Chinese I met to operate equally in both the Chinese community and the greater-Houston non-Chinese community. Yet, I never thought it was my place to tell him that fence-sitting would only garner him splinters.

VII

The Ghost of China Past

The Indian writer V.S. Naipaul traveled to the land of his ancestors for the first time when he was 30-years-old. He was born in Trinidad and went to England on a scholarship when he was 18. As the descendant of 19th-century indentured Indian emigrants, his nascent Caribbean circumstances and subsequent intermediate immigration are similar to many of the Chinese in this country today.

When he took that initial trip to India in 1962 he knew a feeling of alienation, a feeling so different about and from the "India" of his youth. "I grew up with two ideas of India. The first idea—not one I wanted to go into too closely—was about the kind of country from which my ancestors had come. We were an agricultural people. Most of us in Trinidad were still working on the colonial sugar estates, and for most of us life was poor; many of us lived in thatched, mud-walled huts. Migration to the New World, shaking us out of the immemorial accepting ways of peasant India, had made us ambitious; but in colonial and agricultural Trinidad, during the Depression, there were few opportunities to rise. With this poverty around us, and with this sense of the world as a kind of prison (the barriers down against us everywhere), the India from which my ancestors had migrated to better themselves became in my imagination a most fearful place. This India was private and personal, beyond the India I read about in newspapers and books. This India, or this anxiety about where we had come from, was like a neurosis.

"There was a second India. It balanced the first. This second India was the India of the independence movement, the India of the great names. It was also the India of the great civilization and the great classical past. It was the India by which, in all the difficulties of our circumstances, we felt supported. It was an aspect of our identity, the community identity we had developed, which, in multi-racial Trinidad, had become more like a racial identity.

"This was the identity I took to India on my first visit in 1962. And when I got there I found it had no meaning in India. The idea of an Indian community—in effect, a continental idea of our Indian identity—made sense only when the community was very small, a minority, and isolated. In the torrent of India, with its hundred of millions, where the threat was of chaos and the void, that continental idea was no comfort at all. People needed to hold on to smaller ideas of who and what they were; they found stability in the smaller groupings of region, clan, caste, family.

"They were groupings I could hardly understand. They would have given me no comfort at all in Trinidad, would have provided no balance for the other India I carried as a neurosis, the India of poverty and an abjectness too fearful to imagine," (Naipaul 1990:7-8).

This anxiety, this neurosis Naipaul developed from the ghost of India played upon him, fed into his forming an identity and shifting that identity again, like the tide pulling the unstable foundation of sand from the Caribbean beaches. India, the physical country existed; he could travel to that. But in Trinidad, as the grandson and great-grandson of agricultural immigrants, he had grown up with his own ideas of the distance that separated him from India. "I was far enough away form it to cease to be of it. I knew the rituals but couldn't participate in them; I heard the language, but followed only the simpler words. But I was near enough to understand the passions; and near enough to feel my own fate was bound up with the fate of the people of the country. The India of my fantasy and heart was something lost and irrecoverable," (ibid.:491).

Like Naipaul, the Chinese also know the atavistic comfort of family, clan, and region. But unlike Naipaul, the people in my study have no consternation with the presence of their past. Comparatively, Amy Tan's heroine Kwan, in *A Hundred Secret Senses*, never "leaves" China during the lengthy time she remains in the States (Tan 1995). China is a unifying presence in her life; and Kwan, Tan says, believes that she and her American half-sister are "connected by a cosmic Chinese umbilical cord" that has given them "the same inborn traits, personal motives, fate, and luck," (ibid.:21).

Kwan has *yin* eyes which see ghosts in the present time she lives as well as in the past of China. These are Chinese ghosts, and "foreigners" don't believe in them. In the States, her ghost-sitings and citings land her in a mental hospital where Kwan undergoes shock treatment and subsequently retains so much electricity in her body that supernatural tendencies (of acting and thinking) are attributed to her (Or, is it to the ghosts?). In her seemingly unbounded ability to retain and recall dreams, she is constantly confronted with difference and the need to reconcile a meaning with her present life. In one case, she recalls seeing her first foreigner around the time opium was clearing an undermining highway through China: "When foreigners arrived in our province, everyone in the countryside—from Nanning to Guilin—talked about them. Many Westerners came to trade in foreign mud, the opium that gave foreigners mad dreams of China. And some came to sell weapons—cannons, gunpowder, rifles, not the fast, new ones, but the slow, old kind you light with a match, leftovers from foreign battles already lost. The missionaries came to our province because they heard that the Hakkas were God Worshippers. They wanted to help more of us go to their heaven. They didn't know that a God Worshipper was not the same as a Jesus Worshipper. Later we all realized our heavens were not the same," (ibid.:32).

But the foreigner Kwan met was not a missionary. He was an American military leader, "a supreme general" of the "highest rank." "He was a God Worshipper himself, and he admired us, our laws against opium, thievery, the pleasures of the dark parts of women's bodies. . . .He said that he had come to help us win our battle against the Manchus, that this was God's plan, written more than a thousand years before in the Bible he was holding. People pushed forward to see. We knew that same plan. The Heavenly King had already told us that the Hakka people would inherit the earth and rule God's Chinese kingdom," (ibid.:33).

Implicit in the definition of an immigrant is that one has a less rooted feeling for one's homeland. But for the Chinese, as illustrated by Tan's fictional character Kwan, physical migration does not separate one from the influence of one's historical consciousness and cultural unconsciousness. Honoring the strength of their traditions is central to the lives of Chinese. It is their connection through shared memory and knowledge of the past—and many have said it's the confidence in the superiority of their own culture—that legitimates their present social order. "When tradition is concrete, when it is a part of life, sacred, something to be feared and loved, then it takes the form of ghosts," Fei wrote after visiting the United States in the mid-1940s (Fei 1989:177).

It is this significant connection through the past visiting the present that attends to creating coherent transmission for the Chinese culture. Ghosts for the Chinese are not always the scary concoctions of American Halloween nor the catalysts of clinical psychotherapeutic treatment. A more serious consideration is that they are ties of kinship between the old and the new, signifying succession and continuity. The ghost stories could indeed be scary to very young children who had no comprehension of the dead visiting their lives. But more importantly, ghost stories such as those told to Kingston as well as the ghost-sitings of Fei close whatever gap could exist between generations.

Fei's story of the first time he saw a ghost creates an understanding of the position family attachment continues to have in the lives of the Chinese. It happened that he saw the ghost of his grandmother, who had lived with Fei and his family, in the same year that she died. "One day not long after her death, I was sitting in the front room looking toward her bedroom. It was almost noon. Normally at that time Grandmother would go to the kitchen to see how the lunch preparations were coming along, soon after which lunch would be served. This had been a familiar sight for me, and after her death the everyday pattern was not changed. Not a table or chair or bed or mat was moved. Every day close to noon I would feel hungry. To my subconscious mind the scene was not complete without Grandmother's regular daily routine, and so that day I seemed to see her image come out of her bedroom once more and go into the kitchen. . .At the time I felt nothing unusual, for the scene was so familiar and right. Only a little later when I remembered that Grandmother was dead did I feel upset—not frightened, but sad the way one feels at a loss that should not have occurred. I also seemed to realize that a beautiful scene, once it had existed, would always be. The present loss was just a matter of separation in time, and this separation I felt could be overcome. An inextinguishable revelation had struck; the universe showed a different structure. In this structure our lives do not just pass through time in such a way that a moment in time or a station in life once past is lost. Life in its creativity changes the absolute nature of time: it makes past into present—no, it melds past, present, and future into one inextinguishable, multilayered scene, a three-dimensional body. This is what ghosts are, and not only did I not fear them, I even began to yearn for them," (Fei 1989:178; cf. Chang:194).

Ghosts, then, are in some ways repetitions of familiar scenes, memories worth recalling. But as an American-born Chinese, Kingston's reaction to ghosts stories told by her China-born parents conjured a different kind of reality. Without the same scenery, the same China experience available to her, the China stories became fragments of her family's past and their imagination; and they were imposed on Kingston, embedded in her consciousness to be worked through simultaneously with her ongoing experiences of living in America. A result was that the stories never seemed adequately explained to her, and they made her even more aware of her ethnicity which "is a deeply rooted emotional component of identity," (Fischer 1986:195). This experience brings home forcefully for immigrants the paradoxical sense that "ethnicity is something reinvented and reinterpreted in each generation by each individual and that it is often something quite puzzling to the individual, something over which he or she lacks control. Ethnicity is not something dynamic, often unsuccessfully repressed or avoided," (ibid.). Kingston writes, "Those of us in the first American generations have had to figure out how the invisible world the emigrants built around our childhoods fits in solid America. . .Chinese-Americans, when you try to understand what things in you are Chinese, how do you separate what is peculiar to childhood, to poverty, insanities, one family, your mother who marked your growing with stories, from what is Chinese? What is Chinese tradition and what is the movies?" (Kingston 1989:5-6).

The ghost stories were supposed to teach moral lessons, were supposed to be examples of one's duty and the consequences of abjuring one's responsibility to the community. But for Kingston, stories of her "aunt, my forerunner" fit incongruently in her imagination: "Unless I see her life branching into mine, she gives me no ancestral help," (ibid.:8). Ghosts began to take a different shape for Kingston; since ghosts became metarelationship for her, since she found herself aware of her ethnicity by comparison with her past and her present, all those non-Chinese around her became "ghosts" who could not be trusted with family secrets whose telling could get the family sent back to China (ibid.:163-209).

Being Chinese on the mainland, or on Taiwan, or in Hong Kong—or anyplace which is predominantly ethnic Chinese—is complex; but being Chinese in America has additional complicating features. An effort to "take" with them what was "left" behind is realized in the desire to remember and in the means to reproduce from that memory. Many mirrors (always devices of distortion) are employed to create a composite image of meaning (Wang Gungwu:135-136; cf. Yang 1994).

Richard Rorty calls this imaging through the use of mirrors inaccurate and optional; the imagery of the Mirror of Nature is a *presence* and not necessarily an object which is identical in substance to what is represented (Rorty 1979). For example, the reflection visible in the water or in the mirror or in the chrome of the car's bumper is not a case of the subject becoming identical with the object anymore than it is to view a Chinese living in America and call him *American*. As Rorty says, if we hold consciousness apart from reason and from personhood, "then we shall no longer be tempted by the notion that knowledge is made possible by a special Glassy Essence which enables human beings to mirror nature. Thus we shall not be tempted to think that the possession of an inner life, a stream of consciousness, is relevant to reason. Once consciousness and reason are separated out in this way, then personhood can be seen for what I claim it is—a matter of decision rather than knowledge," (Rorty:37-38).

What Stephen A. Tyler says of ethnography—that is to say, "evocation"—as being the discourse of the post-modern world can be applied to reconceptualizing Chinese identity: "Evocation is neither presentation nor representation. It presents no objects and represents none, yet it makes available through absence what can be conceived but not presented. It is thus beyond truth and immune to the judgment of performance. It overcomes the separation of the sensible and the conceivable, of form and content, of self and other, of language and the world," (Tyler 1986:123; cf. Tyler 1978:164-166). And "since evocation is nonrepresentational, it is not to be understood as a sign function, for it is not a 'symbol of,' nor does is 'symbolize' what it evokes," (Tyler 1986:129).

So if Tyler's point is that by "evoking" rather than "representing," ethnography (our "thoughts" about our subject) is freed from mimeses, then I assert that identity among the Chinese immigrants I study—those who maintain an active participation in traditional cultural standards and revisionist thinking concerning their national and political boundaries—is not the subject of a mirror but is rather a restructuring of connectedness to their cultural inheritance. In the course of my fieldwork in Houston, I was continually reminded of the unbridgeable distinction made by Chinese between being Chinese and being American. For the younger ones especially, their cultural—as well as ethnic—identity supersedes a sense of physical origins. It incorporates belonging to a social structure with certain norms of conduct. And that differs from the Western (American) individual so disconnected by plethora of simultaneous relationships which privilege the competition of self *vs* another self. As M. M. Bakhtin writes of relations, "The better a person understands the degree to which he is externally determined (his substantiality), the closer he comes to understanding and exercising his real freedom," (Bakhtin 1986:139).

The collective past is drawn upon to contour the present for the Chinese; but in its fixity, the past is in no way the absolute subject over which the present is traced for the Evergreen students in my study. Bakhtin's analysis of the epic and the novel as literary genres are particularly useful metaphors for purposes of discerning the differences between (epic) historically-shaped identity and (novel) imagined responses. The poetics as well as the peculiarities of the novel set it distinctively apart from the epic. Writing that the study of the novel as a genre is distinguished by certain difficulties that are "due to the unique nature of the object itself: the novel is the sole genre that continues to develop, that is as yet uncompleted. The forces that define it as a genre are at work before our very eyes: the birth and development of the novel as a genre takes place in the full light of the historical day. The generic skeleton of the novel is still far from having hardened, and we cannot foresee all its plastic possibilities.

"We know other genres, as genres, in their completed aspect, that is, as more or less fixed pre-existing forms into which one may then pour artistic experience. The primordial process of their formation lies outside historically documented observation. We encounter the epic as a genre that has not only long since completed its development, but one that is already antiquated. With certain reservations we can say the same for the other major genres, even for tragedy. The life they have in history, the life with which we are familiar, is the life they have lived as already completed genres, with a hardened and no longer flexible skeleton. Each of them has developed its own canon that operates in literature as an authentic historical force," (Bakhtin 1981:3).

These words of Bakhtin are particularly useful, because his metaphors of the epic and the novel parallel the project of deconstructing identity formation and expression: exploring the tensions between ascribed historical origins and created beginnings, between official discourse of the parents and teachers, and socially contingent meanings of the Houston (Western) environment in which the younger Chinese immigrants are growing up. His epic-novel comparison is not unlike other venues in transition with cross-cultural dialectics and developing identities. Whereas an established history and sanguinal traditions are advantageous to perpetuate facts and myths, an evolving culture which is creating new identities with and within each new generation is unfolding beyond, even in spite of, the established Chinese traditions. As Bakhtin says of the differences between the epic and the novel as two significant literary genres, they are affected by a very specific rupture in (European) civilization, and the formerly historically-based theories and methods of identity formation must submit to new scrutiny. The same application can be made to these Chinese immigrants.

The epic as a genre is characterized by three features: the absolute past; a national tradition (not personal experience and the free thought that grows out of it); and the absolute distance which separates the epic world from contemporary reality. "The world of the epic is the national heroic past: it is a world of 'beginnings' and 'peak times' in the national history, a world of fathers and of founders of families, a world of 'firsts' and 'bests.' The important point here is not that the past constitutes the content of the epic. The formally constitutive feature of the epic as a genre is rather the transferal of a represented world into the past, and the degree to which this world participates in the past," (ibid.:13). The world of history and of the epic, therefore, is behind the younger Chinese with its own canon. "The epic world is an utterly finished thing, not only as an authentic event of the distant past but also on its own terms and by its own standards; it is impossible to change, to re-think, to re-evaluate anything in it. It is completed, conclusive and immutable, as a fact, an idea and a value," (ibid.:17).

By comparison, the novel, like contemporary locations of Chinese identity formation and expression, had from the very beginning (for the novel, during the late Middle Ages and Renaissance) a new way of conceptualizing time and space (chronotope). The absolute past, tradition, and hierarchical distance characteristic of the epic had no role in the formation of the novel as genre. From the very beginning the novel was structured not in the distanced image of the absolute past but in the zone of direct contact with inconclusive present-day reality. At its core lay personal expression and free creative imagination," (ibid.:39).

The exilic immigrant is a special case of someone whose identity endures a maelstrom of circumstances often unforeseen, or at least unanticipated to the extent that one suddenly is thrust into the uncertainty of forced relocation. Traditionally, "exile" is taken to mean banishment by governments for a particular crime and for a particular time (often for life). Usually, the application is to a physical removal, but exile can be an internal expression as well. Naficy's attention to the exilic Iranian liminar is devoted mostly to those in the Los Angeles area, the largest such community in the United States, and to their most visible means of producing and consuming information and knowledge: television and film media. It is by these means that the exile discourse on nostalgia and the syncretic space of liminality is most far-reaching and appealing in its attempt to reconstruct something out of memory or nothing. Naficy's particular definition of exile is a palimpsest inscribed with many layers of meanings, deeply rooted in the culture and psyche of Iranians (Naficy 1993:149). For him, the exile is so far beyond the touchstone of original contact that all memory has been partially or completely obliterated; thus, the exilic liminal discourse is an attempt to recreate, and its product can be illusory. Like the Chinese, the exile wants to take with him what he remembers leaving behind; but the difference between the two groups lies in the insecure space of liminality, a state of unbelonging and hybridization. Syncretism and hybridity are similar in some respect, Naficy says, but they are by no means the same. "Syncretism involves impregnating one culture with the contents of another in order to create a third, stable culture while hybridity involves an ambivalence about both of the original cultures, thereby leading to creation of a slipzone of indeterminacy and shifting positionalities," (ibid.:127). This state of unbelonging, he continues, is "in effect a form of freedom, nomadism, homelessness, or vagrancy—even opportunism—because it settles on nothing but difference itself. The dominant host culture does not interpellate the exiles unproblematically. Host-exile power relations produce psychological and ideological ambivalences that, when unresolved into syncretism, can lead to defensive hybrid strategies of disavowal, self-deception, fetishization of the homeland, nostalgic longing, and chauvinistic nationalism," (ibid.).

V. S. Naipaul tells us that "most of us know the parents or grandparents we come from. But we go back and back, forever; we go back all of us to the memories of thousands of beings," (Naipaul 1994:11). Naficy realized the dualism of return (actually and in created memory) 13 years after he left Iran, the same year the revolution removed the shah. His plane touched the tarmac one warm August evening near midnight. The air was so incredibly thick and warm "that it had become a material thing into which I stepped. Ghosts of other planes seemed to silently float in that dark thickness like grey whales in water. . .I did not know whether my name would be on the list kept by the airport security and this began to gnaw at me as passengers lined up for the first of what turned out to be four checkpoints. At the first, the customs agent asked what the address of my residence in Iran would be. For a moment I panicked because I could not remember the house number. I told him I had been away for many years and could not remember it. My candor brought a smile to his face. 'How about 280' he said. Considerably relieved, I said: 'That'll do.' He entered the fictitious address on the form. This was my first encounter with the Iran I knew, and the first of many realizations that the monolithic monster the exiles in Los Angeles had created of the current Iran was a much more nuanced and complex organism. I felt at home, realizing at the same time that not all people—especially not those on various blacklists—would be treated so kindly. On learning how long I had been away, the last agent waved me on without checking my luggage, saying: 'Welcome to your homeland, enjoy your time.' I felt welcomed, simultaneously realizing in the treatment of returnees the Islamic government's attempt to reverse the loss of skilled people caused by the revolution and by its own subsequent policies.

"My sister Nahid had given a party to celebrate my arrival. After the party, upon leaving her house, the atmosphere was somehow charged as if I was leaving the country. Earlier that night my sister's kids had asked me to talk into a tape recorder for them. After relating a few jokes and childhood anecdotes I broke into singing Rumi's famous poem, 'Song of the Reed.' I began hesitatingly but my voice gradually gained confidence. Emboldened, I closed my eyes and abandoned myself to the exilic lament of the poem and was amazed at how much of it I was able to recall after so many years. At a few points I forgot the lines and paused, but my father who was sitting near me quickly fed them to me. In the end, I opened my eyes to see that I was not the only one overwhelmed with tears. The bittersweet realization came to me again that return can never be fully consummated. To be sure, I had returned, and was with my loved ones again, but it was temporary and, besides, we were in the grip of other exiles. If exile be palimpsest, I had reached only one layer. Many more remained," (Naficy 1993:125-126).

Stuart Hall, who writes about Third World cinema and the emergent subject in the new cinema of the Caribbean, asserts that identity is never a finished thing; it is neither found completely in the past, positioned within completed narratives. Identity does have stable, unchanging, and continuous frames of reference, but identity is not static in this sedulous oneness. Different from Naficy's palimpsest, which is in layers but can be completely or partially erased, is another means of considering how the past can influence the present or at least serve as a developmental stage; it is an interesting phenomenon of oil paintings which reveals—only in the process of age/time—how the artist originally inscribed the canvas. The English word for this effect is pentimento, and it is appropriated from the Italian word for repentance.

Characteristically, painters first make an underpainting or drawing on the same canvas for which the finished work is planned. These are the first thoughts transferred from the author to the medium. Either these original lines are maintained as a model, or they are transmuted in a later attempt before the "real" painting is made with oils. For example, a halo above a saint in a Renaissance painting may be redrawn; or the bend in a child's elbow may move; or the attitude produced by the thrust of another's chin may be completely subverted to appearances that the tax collector is actually a humble sort of man. But regardless of the artist's final work on the canvas, his last layer of paint, the process of oxidation and environmental change can eventually reveal his first thought; and further, the pentimento distinguishes his original work of art from subsequent copies, because the original will always be inscribed with traces of the earliest work and any alterations made to it.

The point here is that pentimento is a window into the mutable thoughts of the artist; and the effect grants us, the spectators, the view of ideas which blur, blend, and reform to produce the present work. As a trace of an earlier composition which becomes visible with the passage of time, pentimento is revelatory of first thoughts with provision for further thoughts, for re-pentance, for re-thinking. Like the artist's pentimento, the Chinese in my study are reconceptualizing and reappraising their identity in a perspective which we can consider as blurring their boundaries between the past and the present.

Too often critics who want to examine and define the construction and expression of identity mistakenly compartmentalize a culture, the individual, and his metonymic representation. These same writers express juxtapositions bounded within a structural framework; they sometimes separate but overlap units of analysis. I suggest that a more comprehensively expressed analysis of the Chinese is best seen in the textualization of blurred genres, of conflated boundaries. Like the German theorist Hans-Georg Gadamer, I propose that we approach an interpretation of (Chinese) identity with a forestructure of understanding. The "horizon of understanding," Gadamer wrote, continuously changes over the course of history; as one encounters new (textual) material, his current horizons of understanding extend to a "fusion of horizons" which cultural psychologist Kenneth Gergen says does not so much represent an understanding of the text itself as it is "a dialogically derived amalgam of text and forestructure," (Gergen 1991:268).

An examination of identity, particularly as it relates to the Chinese in my study group, requires recognizing that cultural inheritance impacts one's determination and ability to function within the given world. Paul Ricour tells us that re-enactment of the past is an element of survival. Regarding historical knowledge, he says it begins with the way in which we enter into possession of survival and inheritance. Unlike the novel, he writes, the constructions of history are intended to be reconstructions of the past through the notion of "traces". "Inasmuch as it is *left* by the *past*, it *stands* for the past, it "represents" the past, not in the sense that the past would appear itself in the mind (*Vorstellung*) but in the sense that the trace takes place of (*Vertretung*) the past, absent from historical discourse," (Ricour 1984:2). The very act of re-thinking what was once thought is a scandal, Ricour says. Further, the act of taking possession of one's past, not merely inheriting it but claiming it as one's own, "poses anew, in an even sharper way, the question of the survival of the past in the present, without which there would by [sic] no reason to speak of re-enacting, rethinking, or re-creating," (ibid.:12). Similarly, Hall's comments on the subject's identity in new cinema are that identity should not be grounded in archaeology but in re-telling the past, not in re-discovery but in production.

Traditionally, the Chinese have a harmonious impulse toward organizing their lives. Although their political history has been punctuated with upheavals and transitions to successive dynasties, a sense of continuity and "proximity" to the "homeland" is imprinted on the Chinese through efforts within their families and in the Chinese community through efforts such as Evergreen. The young Chinese I studied had no sense of loss of their culture. In fact, they have a deep sense of *belonging* to their culture, and their identity stems from that belonging. Although the landscape of their parents' and these kids' earlier lives is different, a chance of maintaining an identity through language and through association with other Chinese are the imputei to keeping intact a sense of themselves as different from the non-Chinese of Houston.

I think it is because of this *sameness* that until I asked questions of my informants that caused them to think deeply and consciously about their commitment to having a Chinese identity, for the most part they were unable to answer simple questions such as, "What is it like to be Chinese in Houston?" It was not unusual for me to find that it took one or two more meetings before my informants, the younger ones especially, could begin to put words to an answer. Indeed, on several occasions when I would query adult informants and make comments on observations I had made about Chinese attitudes and responses to social situations, these acquaintances would look puzzled, smile and say, "You know, I never thought before you mentioned (this or that about) it. I guess it's just the Chinese way (to respond or behave in a certain manner). I am Chinese, and I live my life as I am accustomed. You're different, and you notice these things." (cf. Tyler 1978:83).

Occasionally, however, I would hear something like "Oh, it's great," as one high school senior eagerly responded one afternoon. "We can talk to each other in Chinese and the others don't know what we're saying!" This "secret language" formed a trans-ethnic bond with "white" students who asked their Chinese friends how to curse in Mandarin in front of their teachers.

"Yes, they have the best of both worlds," a mother of one of these students responded when I related the girl's comments.

"That's right. They do," another mother in the room agreed.

Still, there were others I encountered who thought speaking with me was a chance to vent their frustration about their peers who didn't keep the traditions in as pure a form as the frustrated speakers would intend: "My culture is like the blood in my veins," a high school senior told me one day. As she spoke, she raised her right arm away from her body, bending her elbow so that her forearm was raised upward, and gestured to the veins in that forearm as if she were pointing out her Chinese blood. I couldn't help but recognize that her gesture resembled so much the effort one makes to show strength and prowess.

"It's important to keep the Chinese traditions," she said very firmly, "but so many people in Taiwan and here are becoming Westernized. They value European art and music and languages; they think being known as speaking a Western language makes them more important."

Her sister, who attended the same class and shared a strong sense of Chinese identity formed as much from her cultural milieu as from the opposition she encountered from non-Chinese at her Houston-area high school, overheard our conversation and added, "If we (Asians) try to be friends with white kids at our school, those kids call us Wannabe Whites. So, I usually hang out with ABCs, and then the white kids call us FOBs."

"What's that?!" I asked.

"They say we're Fresh Off the Boat."

A Conscious Choice of Identity

VIII
Identity Claimed—Not Merely Inherited

"In a life with many turnings, there are fragments of memory that return and retreat," Dore Ashton writes in her biography *About Rothko* (1983:5). "Certain fixed images that have somehow withstood the avalanche of events that overtake a man, seem to have a bearing on his evolution. Rothko carried in him childhood impressions that were ineradicable. He remembered his early family life without enthusiasm, and it would be hard to tell how it affected his life. But the external events that affected his family were deeply graven. When Rothko reminisced about his early childhood he most often recalled the situation, *his* situation, as a Jew among hostile Russians. He did it obliquely: he told of being a child of five and watching, in terror, as Cossacks brandishing their *nagaikas* bore down on him. Those eager to disparage Rothko's self-dramatization are quick to point out that he was born in Dvinsk, one of the most comfortable cities for Jews at the turn of the century . . . Yet, of all the possible memories he could preserve of his first ten years, this is the memory that he most often cited. It could stand for everything else," (Ashton:5-6).

I interject this brief account of Mark Rothko because an Evergreen student's eighth grade art history project renewed my interest in twentieth century European and American art and in so doing created another positional perspective of contemplating identity/difference One day she asked me to help her write a paper as well as make an oral presentation which contrasted the styles and motivation of Georgia O'Keeffe and Käthe Kollwitz. This young girl came from Taiwan only four years earlier and had never been exposed to much knowledge of any art except that of the Chinese (which includes the tradition of subordinating the human characters to the grandeur of landscapes). I asked her if she had visited any of the local galleries and museums (including the Rothko Chapel which houses fourteen lording monochrome canvases in an austere presence of enormous silence). "No," was her reply. But she expressed that she wants to study art when she is older and makes her own decisions about how she spends her time. I encouraged her to visit the chapel and gave her much of the following information.

One of the most intriguing confrontations upon entering the Rothko Chapel from the park outside near the small campus of the University of St. Thomas is the hushed, self-controlled environment, as opposed to the free, unconstrained, public environment just outside the chapel's heavy doors. Immediately in front of the chapel is a reflecting pond which hosts Barnett Newman's 26-foot high steel sculpture, *Broken Obelisk*. Turning from that to face the chapel, one sees "no steps, no portico, no column, no crucifixes, no statuary, no spire, no dome, no stained glass, no *windows*—just a low, simple entrance with two black, wood doors. Plain, cheerless, geometric, with in interior sealed off from the pleasant neighborhood and park outside, the building looks more like a tomb than a chapel or one-man museum," (Breslin 1993:463).

As soon as someone enters the antechamber, one's voice conforms to whispered exchanges (that is, if one still feels compelled to speak. But few words are spoken.). Urban sociologist Richard Sennett's description of Western culture as one "given to interiors," applies to the contemplative space of the chapel. "The reason the interior has endured as a space of inner life is that this visual dimension seems to promise spiritual, or as we would now say, subjective freedom—more freedom of reflection and feeling and self-searching than is possible among the contingencies of the street. In our culture, the free play of subjective life seems to require an enclosed environment rather than an exposed one," (Sennett 1990:244).

Since Rothko's chapel design and the dominating canvases he painted for it were completed in the period just before the end of his life, it is interesting to consider that his own material journey from pre-revolutionary Russia to the United States strangely paralleled a spiritual voyage from his childhood during which he was schooled and prayed in Hebrew to his adult years in which he did not identify himself with being Jewish yet refused to consider exhibiting his work in Germany because of that country's atrocities toward the Jews during the Holocaust. Rothko read the early Patristic Fathers, particularly the fourth century Alexandrian theologian Origen, when he was a young man and later painted a number of canvases depicting seminal Christian events: a Last Supper, a Crucifixion, and Gethsemane. He never converted from Judaism, but he later responded to being asked what the attraction of these writers had been for him: he appreciated "the ballet of their thoughts," and he found in them that thinking "went toward ladders," a comment that was more probably about Rothko's appreciation of the play in Origen's mind rather than Origen's love of God (Ashton:169). We remember that integral to the "ballet" of thoughts of the early Church Fathers was, like the Chinese, their belief in elementary simplicity and their view of the world as being a whole organism. (But unlike the Chinese, the early Fathers were the inheritors of the Greek humanistic tradition.)

What Rothko probably found attractive was to "make East and West merge in an octagonal chapel" of juxtaposing oppositions (ibid.). Like Henri Matisse, before whose *Red Studio* Rothko often passed his days at the Museum of Modern Art, he came to believe that painting was an art of contemplating difference.

A first time visitor to Rothko's chapel is likely to feel stunned or subdued in the austere presence of the enormous silence and the fourteen lording monochrome canvases, some of which stretch as high as 15 feet on the walls. The light is quiet but often uneven; and the only furnishings are four wooden benches set equidistant from one another and in front of the paintings, four tall iron and wood candelabra, and a few round black cushions able to be moved about on the floor for individual seating. The space is truly focused on the paintings. With sameness all about him, his masterful paintings of the grid were means to self-transmute the individual meditating before the canvases. Rather than create an environment which would confuse and annoy the visitor, Rothko intended the chapel to be a space of contemplation, an environment which could transport the viewer into a space greater than the painted canvases themselves. Tibetan Buddhist scholar and oft-

lecturer on Buddhist art Robert Thurman tells his audiences that the
Buddha considered art to be sacred because it caused a viewer to be
lifted out of his self (-centeredness) and into contemplation beyond
oneself. It is not unusual, therefore, to hear someone compare Rothko's
work with Zen Buddhist meditation. Indeed, Rothko's "hunger for
illumination, for personal enlightenment, for some direct experience—
or at least the quality of that experience—with the transcendent" was a
leitmotif in his life's work (Ashton:194).

Ashton writes of Rothko's inventing a tradition, a place where he
could find a style with which he could identify: "Every artist seeks or
creates a tradition within which he can feel unique. Rothko had to
invent a tradition, or a fiction of a tradition, because it is only in the
contents of a life of the mind, that includes every place it has wandered,
that an artist can find his style. Sometimes he must abandon his present
in order to find it again and test it against the universal human table of
contents he has carried for so many years. Rothko instinctively sought
another context," (Ashton:170).

Finding oneself transformed by distance and culture at a very
young age may seem like a maelstrom for anyone, particularly someone
so young, who searches for sameness among so much difference.
Without a rooted feeling, one encounters dispossession that exceeds
merely losing or at least eliminating a great deal of one's physical
possessions. The loss challenges the very centeredness of one's
identity. As one contemplates the difference over and over again, one
risks feeling more alienated from a sameness, an identity.

The Chinese of whom I'm writing have had no need to invent the
source of identity that, as Ashton suggest, may have been Rothko's
effort to express. Like the Chinese at Evergreen, Rothko was
transplanted into an Other-wise dominant culture in an act of rupture,
which, especially for children who have no voice in the family decision
to leave—nor in the choice of staying—is a means of severing one from
one's native place. For Rothko, this meant that in "America, he had
been liberated from czarist oppression, but he also had been removed
from his flat, his street, his school, his town, from relatives and close
friends, from his language, his culture, his climate; all of these, no
matter how oppressive or frightening they sometimes felt, were now
lost," (Breslin:43). But unlike the Chinese whose studies of their

language and culture are elegiac to their heritage and testimonies to their (collective) identity, Rothko's mutable life's work may simply have been an effort to correct dissonance he encountered in differences. As Hannah Arendt said of the exiles who, in the foreign place to which they had traveled, must get beyond the memory of terror and regret as well as nostalgia, the challenge to eliminating their sense of loss was to invent the conditions of their own and their common lives. No identity could be recovered; therefore, they needed to turn outwardly (Sennett:130).

If we accept Arendt's explanation we might more easily understand the ambiguities which existed in Rothko's life's work and showed some kinship with the past created by him rather than the past inherited by him. For example, his cavernous New York studio where he designed the chapel and the murals had a concrete floor and a skylight from which he was shielded by a parachute silk. "His love for familiar surroundings was such that he wanted also to have the same cement floor, and the same kind of walls," in the chapel, Dominique de Menil later recalled (*Art Journal* 1971:249). Even the suggestion of the parachute on the ceiling was made—most likely at the expense of a better lighting design to accommodate the searing Texas heat and sun's angle that bore down on the roof of the chapel so relentlessly and differently from the New York position.

Regardless, it is our consideration of his providing us with the means of *contemplating* difference and sameness in the Rothko Chapel that most interest us. His "love for familiar surroundings" did not include anything related to a nascent Jewish identity, yet by contemplating difference and surrounding himself with the comfort of the familiar, he lay claim to an identity. While some immigrants throughout the world, eager to be accepted in their new setting, try to conform to doing "as the Romans do," it is clear that Chinese identity is not shaped by external attempts to categorize it. In all cases of my study group, not only did the students exhibit unquestioned similitude with a Chinese identity, they saw their appropriating whatever Western things they found attractive not only uncontradictory, but also reflective of a desire to act on the mandate of choice. The Chinese, comfortable in their familiar customs and in the knowledge of their large numbers who have honored basic customs for hundreds of generations, are plainly confronted here with non-Chinese difference. For me, it was always an affirmation of their identity to listen to them talk about themselves within the greater Houston setting of the West so different from the China of their past.

Tyler reminds us that some ethnographers make dialogue the focus of their work; and those people are in a sense correct, because "dialogue *is* the source of the text, but dialogue rendered as text, which must be the consequence, is no longer dialogue, but a text masquerading as a dialogue, a mere monologue about a dialogue since the informant's appearances in the dialogue are at best mediated through the ethnographer's dominant authorial role," (Tyler 1987:66). Tannen's concern that style differences work to the disadvantage of those in the subordinate position are actually echoes of Tyler's assertion seven years earlier when he wrote that "while it is laudable to include the native, his position is not thereby improved, for his words are still only instruments of the ethnographer's will. And if the dialogue is intended to protect the ethnographer's authority by shifting the burden of truth from the ethnographer's words to the natives' it is even more reprehensible, for no amount of invoking the 'other' can establish *him* as the agent of the words and deeds attributed to him in a record of dialogue unless he too is free to reinterpret it and flesh it out with caveats, apologies, footnotes, and explanatory detail (*per contra* Crapanzano 1980). These, then, are not dialogues, but sophistic texts like those pretenses at dialogue perpetrated by Plato. The test of true dialogue is that when it is captured in text or recording it is almost incomprehensible, a thing of irruptions and interruptions, of fits and starts, thoughts strangled halfway to expression, dead ends, wild shifts, and sudden inexplicable returns to dead and discarded topics. No, the meaning of the dialogue is not in the dialogue any more than it is in the clever text of a dialogue; it is instead in what the participants make of it separately and in concert, at that time and on later reflection," (ibid.).

I am keenly aware that the following texts of conversations with some of my informants exist because I, mostly, wished that they exist; I engaged my informants in conversation, and these are the results. Certainly, the opposition of sameness and difference is an illusion, not unlike the illusion Aristotle demonstrated when he sought to make tropes functions of the text alone; oppositions are actually dependencies, creating the environment for distinctions between same and different.

JOYCE

She is seventeen years old; and in the last nine months Life has accosted her with more sink or swim, fail or survive challenges than many people experience all their long lives. She was born in Taiwan and spent much or her formative life in Panama. Four years earlier she moved to Houston with her mother, her four-year-old sister, and her father, who traveled most of the time. They settled in the far southwest part of Houston outside of the city limits near where so many other Chinese live, but they moved just next door to the school district where Joyce could have attended with many other Asians. She wished to be perceived as Chinese, and she was deeply disappointed to have few people at her school with whom to share this identity. As Joyce, speaking in a "rapid fire" and emotional delivery, later told me during the winter of her junior year of high school, "There are only two other Asians there: one ABC and one born in Taiwan but who has lived here nearly all her life. They don't speak Chinese. I can't be friends with them. They don't understand that I want to speak Chinese. It's my language. It's my culture. I tell my parents that I don't feel like I fit in at school. They just say, 'Try to fit in. Try to get along with the others.' They don't understand how I feel."

Her mother went to bed complaining of a headache one evening right before Christmas, and she died in her sleep of a massive stroke. Overcome with grief, her father turned his children over to the care of his sister and brother-in-law who also lived in Houston, and he buried himself in his transnational work/travel for the Taiwanese government. A few months later, the aunt and uncle adopted the younger sister, then eight-years-old, and moved to California where the uncle was able to find better work. School had just let out for the summer, and Joyce said she was—unwillingly—going to Gainesville, Florida for the summer to stay with some relatives.

"Why?" she was asked.

"Because they (the aunt and uncle) want to get rid of me. They don't know what else to do with me," she replied, directing her answer to everyone yet to no one in particular.

A few weeks into the fall semester of her senior year, I asked her about her summer and how her year was shaping up. "Florida was awful," she said. "There was nothing to do. I was bored."

I inquired in a general, intentionally-not-so-personal way, about her school year and her living arrangements. Her reply about the school was typical of many like her who aspired to attending college: "I just hate SATs and applying to schools." But her answer to the second part was more startling: "I'm renting a room from a Chinese couple who have two older children away at college."

Amazed that someone so young had taken upon herself so much responsibility, I asked, "Did you know them when you were living with your family?"

"No," was the reply.

"Well, do you think they are all right? Do you feel safe and comfortable?" I asked, trying not to sound anxious.

"Yeah, they're okay," she said.

"I'm awfully sorry that you have no family here, Joyce. You know, my husband and my daughter are the only family I have. Nearly everyone else I'm related to is dead, and I know how difficult that is for a young person," I told her in a feeble way, trying to offer some comradeship.

"Oh, I'm okay. My friends are my family."

And she smiled and continued walking with me to our calligraphy class. For the first time since I had met her—which was shortly after her mother died—I noticed that she stayed beside me as we continued our long walk between classes; every other time I had ever seen her move from one place to another, she had the look of someone who was far more concerned with getting to the next place than having been where she was. This was a different Joyce now, one who was aware of every step she was taking.

Joyce's move to rent a room from strangers stresses the broader drama of her individual isolation. I was very surprised when later the same day that she told me of her new living arrangements she introduced me to a distant cousin (His grandfather and Joyce's grandmother were siblings.) who was the same age and also attending Evergreen. They were friendly but obviously not close. When I later asked her why she didn't live with her cousin and his (her) family, she replied that she had only seen him three times in her life; and besides, he lived in a school district different from hers.

Perhaps renting a room from Chinese strangers was a means of maintaining a cultural bond with her identity while illustrating her emotional distance from her family and the avalanche of events that overtook her and seemingly was having a bearing on her evolution (cf. Ashton's applicable comments on the life of Rothko, Ashton 1983:56). The one absolute in Joyce's life which can shore her against the disruptions of her past and the much greater vicissitudes to come is her sense of *being* Chinese. And for her being Chinese meant tenaciously maintaining a conscious attitude about her Asian features, her mother tongue, and her social activities.

Several weeks later when nearly everyone had dispersed after a long afternoon of classes at Evergreen, I caught up with Joyce as we were walking to the parking lot. We had just come from an after-school meeting that was attended by a lot of Chinese who were Joyce's age but who I didn't know. I had heard a number of them speak before the group, and their English language skills seemed no different from any other young person who has been born and raised in Texas. I also knew that their Chinese language skills were not as good as Joyce's and the others in my usual classroom, because they were not in that same classroom; they were in lower level, less literate groups.

"How are you?" I asked. "I didn't get to talk much with you today."

"I'm fine," she replied. And then she added, "you know, I really look down on these ABCs."

"What do you mean?"

"I just get so irritated with the way they act. And look at the teachers in that meeting. They're not always in control. The kids in there are just wild."

I was accustomed to Joyce's short statements, so I often waited after she made these kind of remarks which were more like punctuations to a conversation rather than sentences. After a few moments of silence, I asked about the status of her life with her host family.

"Oh, it's just *great!*" she said with a big grin. "They are so nice to me!"

"Are you comfortable in the style that they live?" I asked; "Are Chinese traditions important to them?"

"Oh, they're just great! They used to live in Bolivia."

I surmised there was some additional comradeship among them by Joyce and her hosts having lived as Others in Latin countries.

"And do they speak Spanish?"

"Oh, yes. They're fluent."

"So, do you get to practice your Spanish with them at home?"

"No, we speak Chinese all the time."

Before this conversation could develop, especially regarding her comfort in what I hoped was a house that "kept Chinese," she arrived at the side of her car. Seeing that her car key was in her hand, I repeated to her what I had said on a few previous occasions: "Call me if you ever need anything and think I can help you."

"I will. I need your number again. I was going to ask you if you would write a letter of recommendation for me."

"For college?"

"Yes, but I guess I need a teacher's letter."

"Well, I'm happy to do what I can," I said. "I'm sure I can write a letter for you in some capacity of authority."

Certainly this vignette of Joyce which features her truncated family experience is comparatively less common than that of other young people. But her means of coping with her drama highlights an easily recognizable component of Chinese culture which the immigrants in my study emphasized to me in every response to my two-part inquiry, "What is the source of your inspiration for retaining a Chinese identity? And what is essential about being Chinese (in Houston)?"

The answer to a lesser extent was a fellowship of race and the accompanying conviction of having an assumed common origin. The greater resource was a sense of connection, of personal responsibility (duty) to continuing a long-standing tradition of interdependence. For those in my study raised in a family which emphasized the Chinese tradition of bringing honor to the family and always avoiding bringing shame, there carried the conviction of behaving humbly. For those I observed to have been in Houston most of their memorable lives, there was less a concern about humility; but their sense of connection remained, underwritten in a large part by their Chinese language studies and their family's encouragement to have Chinese friends.

So while Joyce's tragic personal experiences differed from the other Evergreen students, her identity with ethnic and cultural sameness helped to repair and strengthen her in the face of differing circumstances. Joyce is very diligent in all the work she undertakes, so it is not surprising that she has an excellent academic record. She also extends herself in a busy schedule of after-school youth activities at Evergreen as well as with the Spanish club and the senior class projects at her high school. But Joyce's career choice may signal more than a young person's ambition for a satisfying profession. I find it somewhat bittersweet that in the face of the violated personal connections which underlie her identity, which have threatened to undermine the (cultural and social) connection she was raised to expect as well, Joyce is avoiding a career that would bring her into close personal contact with others: Joyce's plan is to become a veterinarian.

JIMMY

"Overseas Chinese" is the categorical reference to those people in diaspora as well as to children born of Chinese parents who choose a permanent settlement outside of Taiwan or the mainland. The reference is an interesting one, because it implies these people's real home is China.

Most of the subjects in my study came from Taiwan. Although there are those who believe that the island itself is a country and challenge the long-standing belief in the unity of a Chinese culture, nation, and state, nevertheless "they identify themselves as Chinese—which they see as a cultural or ethnic designation—while identifying themselves as citizens of Taiwan," (Wachman:22). They speak of their lineage or heritage (*xue tong*), "acknowledging their acceptance of a 'blood relationship' to Chinese from the mainland while rejecting the idea that all Chinese must live under the same government within the same polity. They reject the idea of a Chinese nation-state. Some even reject the idea of a Chinese nation. Chinese, for them, is a cultural or ethnic category, not a political category," (ibid.).

Politics does, however, enter the equation of disseminating information and influencing identity. With the expressed "view to helping Chinese descendant Youth to enchance [sic] a better understanding of the Chinese cultural [sic] and language, the Overseas Chinese Affairs Commission of the Republic of China on Taiwan sponsors the Overseas Chinese Youth Language Training and Study Tour to the Republic of China annually." This program expresses the desire (evangelism, some might say) of the Nationalist government to have an overseas Chinese youth return "to his motherland" where he "is expected to adjust to Chinese culture and custom," (spring, 1995 letter from Kang-Seng Tsai, Director of the Chinese Culture Center, Taipei Economic and Cultural Office in San Francisco).

A number of Houston Chinese youth have participated in this six-week program which is underwritten by the Taiwanese government and costs only $400 for each of the 900 students to attend four weeks of classes and take a two-week tour of the island. Jimmy is one of them. In the following conversation, he is 21-years-old and a former Evergreen student. He is the only son and second child of parents born in Canton and raised in Taiwan. Jimmy and his sister (who also attended Evergreen and the summer Taiwan youth camp) were born in the United States; and both graduated from the same private high school which is known for high academic standards exacted at the price of a highly competitive environment. The school, once considered to be socially elite because of the high number of wealthy local legacies, is now known for having a broader social and cultural student population. Jimmy now attends a prestigious eastern university and has his sites set on attending medical school next year. I was able to talk to him about his summer experience at the Youth Camp in the very short time he had between arriving from Taiwan and repacking his bags to return to college in August. The following text is a transcription of my hand-written notes of our conversation.

E. Why did you go?

J. Because I thought it would be fun. And it was. Well, at first I didn't want to go because the campus has a bad reputation for being strict and for people getting in trouble for not following the rules. But I had a blast. My sister went the summer after her sophomore year (at Princeton), and I had visited the campus (of the Taiwan youth camp) before. Now I'm really glad I went. I'd like my kids to attend if the program is continued that long.

E. What were your days like there?

J. We attended language classes according to our proficiency level for two hours each morning. The levels were one to twelve, one being the highest. I was a level four, because I could speak fairly well but couldn't read or write as well. Besides the language classes, we could enroll in cultural classes such as martial arts, cooking, kite-making, dance. We also attended a Chinese history class. That was a propaganda thing. The class was about the history of Taiwan, and it covered material only from as far back as when Chiang Kai-shek came with the Nationalists in 1949.

E. Do you know how the kids less proficient in Chinese were able to learn?

J. I think they used a kind of phonetic Roman script like *pinyin* or Wade-Giles.

E. How was the enrollment proportioned by gender?

J. I'd say there were about an equal number of boys and girls, maybe a few more boys than there were girls. There weren't any boys in the dance class, though!

E. What was the primary language of your classmates?

J. Most of them spoke English. We all spoke (Mandarin) Chinese in the classes, but outside of class we spoke English. When we would leave the campus and go into town we would sometimes have to speak Chinese, but we usually spoke English to each other. Most of the kids were from the United States and Canada.

E. Did you improve your Chinese literacy?

J. Yes.

E. Did you have a different sense of being Chinese when you were there?

J. Well, I've been to Taiwan before, and I've been to China. I have relatives in both places. I felt different there. When I was there (in the summer program) I felt more American; but when I am here, I feel more Chinese. I've never joined a Chinese student association because I always thought it was wrong to make friends based on ethnicity; I always thought I should make friends for reasons of their character. And I hardly ever speak Chinese with my friends who are Chinese, because I've always thought it was wrong to speak out loud in another language. I've always thought I should speak English.

E. I know you've been raised in a Chinese-speaking household with Chinese furniture and Chinese art in the formal areas as well as lots of photographs of your family (grandparents, aunts, uncles, parents, and sister) throughout the less formal, more private part of the house. Do you think your homelife with its visible Chinese heritage and language helped you feel more comfortable in the Taiwan summer program?

J. I was more Chinese than most of the Chinese-Americans there.

E. What do you mean by that?

J. All my (Chinese) culture here is second-hand. I was born here, but my parents were born in China, raised in Taiwan, and graduate school-age when they moved to the States. I've been raised here.

E. But I know Chinese is spoken in your home.

J. Well, my mom speaks to me in Chinese. My dad doesn't speak much to me in Chinese. My mom makes me talk to her in Chinese. It's really important to her. It's really hard for me, because sometimes I have something to say that I don't know how to express in Chinese.

E. So why do you feel you were more Chinese than the other students in the program this summer?

J. A lot of them were from California and were very American, very Western.

E. Do you feel the program was supportive of your Chinese identity, or do you feel—as you've already expressed in your opinion that it was "a propaganda thing"—that your time there was largely a political experience?

J. The program was one-sided, very nationalistic. The Taiwanese running the program made a distinction between Taiwan Chinese and mainland Chinese. But we were really pampered. The dorm I stayed in was nice, average like here; there were no squat toilets.

E. How important was it that you attended the training program: would you say your attendance was more important to your parents or that it had equal importance to you and your parents?

J. I'm really glad I went. I went because my parents wanted me to go, and my sister had gone. But I found that it (the summer program) helped me to find more of my Chinese identity, heritage. It makes you appreciate it (the heritage). I'd like my kids to attend.

MAY AND JENNIFER

These two Chinese will probably never meet. But I include them together, because each in her way have worked vigorously toward claiming the Chinese identity formerly denied them. May is nearly 70-years-old and from Hong Kong; Jennifer is 17 and from Taiwan. Each find themselves in Houston under circumstances that were not their choosing, but each has taken the turnings in their lives to find a new freedom of expressing a Chinese identity out of opposition to the differences they found in their pasts as well as in harmony with the opportunities they find in the Houston Chinese community.

May is a chatty, energetic widow with six grown children. She mentions this and then says with a broad smile, "Number four daughter is unmarried and lives at home with me." This was her way of introducing herself to me the day we met in a Mandarin Chinese class at the Chinese Cultural Center which is sponsored by the Taiwanese government.

May, as well as her parents and her grandparents, were born in Hong Kong. Her marriage was arranged by her aunt with the mother of the prospective groom. The young man who would become her husband was seriously dating an American woman while he was serving in the Chinese army during World War II. The man's father died, and his mother wrote a tearful and desperate letter to the son asking him not to break her heart by marrying the American. The obedient son broke off the romance and returned to Hong Kong right away. Unknown to May, he was sent to a restaurant where she was dining so that he could see what she looked like and observe her manner. Shortly later they officially met (May never having seen him until then), and they dated for three months before their wedding. May and her groom moved to the United States where they operated a grocery for 30 years in the downtown Houston Chinatown. And there they also raised their children who were expected to help in the family business. Ten years ago the family business was sold, and three years later May's husband died.

May never spoke English when she was in Hong Kong. It was only through her husband prodding her to talk to the customers in their business here that she began to learn how to communicate in English. She told me that before she could speak English, she would go to the stores in Houston where she needed to make a purchase and just point to the merchandise she wanted. Now she speaks quite easily and understandably and even quite animatedly.

Since she could read Chinese and spoke the Cantonese dialect, I asked her the day we met why she was taking Mandarin classes once-a-week for the past six years. Her answer illustrates a broader application to claiming a Chinese identity which she always had thought existed for her only in a compromised situation for most of her life:

"I want to understand the friends I'm making who come from Taiwan. My friends tease me now when they are talking among themselves. They know I can understand them better, and they say loudly enough for me to hear, 'Be careful what you are saying now; May is studying Mandarin and can understand us!' I also take a dance class, and I want to understand the teacher's instructions!"

One of the most insightful comments May made to me regarding learning Mandarin had to do with her attitude toward other Chinese immigrants to Houston and her comparative status: "Most of the immigrants here now are from Taiwan, and they have more honor because they are from the old generation. They came from the mainland with the traditional values. The people from Hong Kong are more concerned with making money (The implication, she confirmed, was that the Hong Kong Chinese were more tied to the Western idea of capitalism than they were concerned with living a set of values.)."

"What are the values you're talking about, May?" I asked.

"I've worked hard to teach all my children about respecting one's boss where one worked, because the place where one works, where one is given the opportunity to earn a living, is just like family and should be treated with honor and respect."

She related the story of her unmarried daughter who works two jobs: at Pennzoil and at Foley's, a retail department store. Pennzoil had no knowledge of her dual employment (and would not allow it, according to May's daughter), but Foley's does allow her to work at their company part-time, knowing she is working somewhere else and believing also that two full-time jobs are too demanding on the daughter's time. Foley's had a large lay-off some time ago but kept May's daughter, she said. "They know she has honor and did not turn in false figures for her work time as the colored people did," May explained. Several times she made disparaging remarks about black people as marriage companions, as dishonest workers who didn't accomplish what they were paid to do, and as people who couldn't match the Chinese reputation for being honorable.

May's place of origin is China, albeit a British territory at her birth. But her respect for the people who she saw as caretakers of the best that being Chinese had to offer humbles her while simultaneously inspiring her. She believes that being Chinese is more of a cultural communion and a social practice than it is a political identity. And while being prideful has only a parenthetical place in Chinese culture (as in being proud of one's family and having good self-esteem, but never boasting for oneself), May's acquisition of Mandarin skills and accumulation of Taiwanese friends has greatly enhanced her self-confidence and her happiness of living a Chinese identity within such a large Chinese community. Furthermore, she finds in Houston so many of the amenities which support the life she has fashioned for herself (cultural centers, restaurants, numerous publications, temples and churches, entertainment, libraries, shopping, etc.). Rather than giving into the feeling that she is widowed and living apart from her origins, she finds a connection to a heritage she had always wanted.

Jennifer joined Jack's class half-way through the semester. She asked the kids around her about my being there before I had a chance to introduce myself and came over to me at the first class break time one afternoon.

"I'm Taiwanese Chinese," she said proudly. "My father is seventh generation Taiwanese," she continued. "So you're studying us and our language? Do you know that when I was little my father taught me the Taiwanese dialect; but when I went to school, I was forced to speak only Mandarin. I was stubborn with my teachers there (in Taiwan), and they made me write over and over 'I will not speak Taiwanese.' I had a scar for a long time on my wrist where the teachers hit me for speaking what my father taught me and for not speaking Mandarin. Look, you can still see the little white line where my scar has healed," she told me as she offered up her wrist for me to examine.

Taiwanese and Mandarin are mutually unintelligible. The Taiwan dialect evolved as a variant of the southern linguistic influences in a region of Fukien Province south of the Min River from which most Taiwanese come. "Taiwanese from that region are called *Minnan jen* (people from south of the Min) and the dialect they speak a form of *Minnan jua* (south of the Min speech) which is related to the Hokkien spoken in and around Amoy," (Wachman:107). When the mainlanders came from various provinces in China speaking different regional dialects, they settled on Mandarin, the dialect of the north, as the "national language." As we know from Jennifer's comments, the Kuomintang (KMT) party of the Nationalists enforced a strict policy of using Mandarin for official affairs, in schools, on radio, and on television as part of its effort to re-integrate Taiwan into the Chinese fold. Not only did the KMT mandate that Taiwanese not be spoken; Japanese was forbidden as well. After 1964, when a law was passed by the KMT forbidding the use of Taiwanese in schools or official settings, the autocratic government also launched "a campaign that emphasized the grace of Mandarin and the comparative vulgarity of Taiwanese.

"In schools, speech contests intended to promote fluency in Mandarin caused many Taiwanese to feel inadequate. Taiwanese, which was still the dialect of the home and marketplace, was forbidden in class. It seems every adult Taiwanese who was educated since the KMT arrived recalls the fines, slaps, and humiliations that were meted out as punishment to students heard speaking Taiwanese at school. Taiwanese were made to feel their dialect was somehow less dignified, dirtier, than Mandarin. Taiwanese who spoke Mandarin encumbered with a Taiwanese accent felt vulnerable each time they opened their mouths and ashamed that culturally—and, perhaps, inherently—they were inferior to Mainlanders," (ibid.:108).

Perhaps it is because Jennifer is living with her mother and sister here in Houston only as an opportunity to benefit from Western economic life and to learn to speak English (Her father visits from time to time but prefers to run his southeast Asian business empire from the Pacific rim.), and because Jennifer's parents are very wealthy that Jennifer feels empowered to talk openly about the Taiwanese government she believes spoon-feeds propaganda to its residents. She also obviously carries a great deal of chagrin; because while she is proud of being Chinese and being known as Chinese and having Chinese friends, an atavistic sense of duality gnaws at her.

"There was a scandal in my family when my parents married," she explained to me at our first meeting. "My mother was born in Canton and went to Taiwan with my grandparents when she was only two months old. She grew up in Taipei, but she is Chinese. My father's family were very unhappy that our long Taiwanese line would be mixed by my father's marriage."

"Did your mother learn to speak Taiwanese?" I asked.

"Yes, but she speaks it with an obvious accent. Since we've been here in the States, she has learned to speak some English, but very badly. My dad doesn't speak English at all. But then he's never here for very long. And we speak only Chinese at home and with our friends."

LARRY

He lived nearly all his life in Lesotho, inside South Africa, and moved to Houston the year before we met. He is tall, clean cut with a Western hair style that belies all the other boys' in the classroom (who obviously have Taiwanese barbers who still cut hair like they never left the island!), and has the upright, hands-folded, ankles-crossed posture that I associate with professional dancers. I often see him smiling at comments made by people around him; but I never see him turn and initiate a conversation with another student. Still, he is very approachable and always is prepared to answer questions when called upon in class or when spoken to informally by me or one of the students.

"Is this you first experience attending a Chinese school?" I asked shortly after meeting him.

"No, where we lived in Lesotho there were approximately 300 Chinese. We didn't live together, though; we lived mostly among black Africans. On the weekends we would get together with other Chinese to socialize, and some of us attended a Chinese school there."

"What was that like?"

"It was very rowdy. There were only 20 of us in the school. We were all ages, and we met in the same classroom." He continued to say that he had more of a Chinese identity in that school instead of the Evergreen classroom, because he thought that with so few people there was more emphasis on living and learning Chinese in Africa.

"Did you speak Chinese during the week? At least at home?"

"Oh, yes. We (his two siblings and his parents) always spoke Chinese at home. I went to an international school where I spoke English as well as an African dialect."

"Why did you leave and come here?" I asked.

"Because of the political situation there," he replied. "My father had an import business in South Africa, and he became worried about the future."

"Have you applied to any colleges for next year?" I inquired.

His answers were UCLA, UT (the University of Texas), UC-Berkeley, and Cornell. He is concerned about attending a school which is so competitive. And I ask him whether he would consider applying to a Taiwanese university.

"Oh, no. I don't think I would fit in very well. I speak Chinese well, but I don't write well enough. I couldn't keep up."

"How indicative of Chinese humility," I thought. I had just seen Larry's test score from the last written exam. Not only did he make an "A," he scored one of the highest exams in the room. His particular self-deprecation, I believe, rises from his sense of feeling alien, not only to other Chinese in the greater Houston community of several thousand but also to the larger populations of Chinese in Asia.

"Do your parents encourage you to have good study habits?"

"They used to, but they know now that they don't have to say anything to me. The only thing they say like that is to remind my brother and sister and me at the dinner table at night to be responsible and bring honor to the family."

ROGER

He is a particular exception to the students at Evergreen. He is an ABC from the northeastern part of the United States and is in Houston to attend medical school. Older than the other students and exceptionally fluent in reading and writing Mandarin, Jack lets him drop in when his medical studies permit him the time. Roger speaks English with me, but Jack says that Roger insists on speaking only Chinese with him. It seems that he feels he must constantly hone his skills.

Many anthropological and sociological studies find that it is highly unusual for a second-generation immigrant to lay claim to one's ancestral heritage in the manner of Roger's effort. He, like all the other ABCs and the immigrant youth I talk with, is wholly comfortable with the amenities of Western education and lifestyle comforts they find in this successful capitalistic economy. But Roger wants to *return* to the China of his imagination. He is active in a Chinese student association. He offers prayers at the Jade Buddha Temple as well as seeks companionship in the youth group of the Houston Chinese (Christian) Church, and he wants to study Chinese medical practices in order to create a kind of Sino-Western practice of his own (although he intends to be licensed first in the United States).

For Roger, being Chinese carries an obligation to honor the traditions of his cultural heritage. His attitude toward his parents is never addressed beyond acknowledging that they are proud of his academic achievement and his desire to continue his Chinese language studies. Speaking and studying Chinese is almost a singular crusade for him. He even adopts a long-bangs-in-front, short-shave-in-back hairstyle similar to other male class members from Taiwan and seems a little shy in the manner that many Chinese, embued with their culture, appear to non-Chinese.

IX
Do We Care What Other People Think of Us?

I think it can be said of all Chinese that the first obvious distinction between them and everyone else who is not Chinese is that they look different; their physical appearance undeniably sets them apart. Though few Evergreen students in my class were aware of—or at least admitted to—being teased for their "slanted" eyes, the older college-age students who were either born and raised in the States or had lived here most of their memorable lives did recall being made to feel different; "Yeah, kids would tease me," an ABC student from a community with few Asians recalled, "but I knew I was smart and funny, could be a friend and have friends. I didn't let it bother me. My home life was different from my (non-Chinese) friends, but then I guess I just accepted that we did things differently in my house."

The second distinguishing quotient, as young Chinese become aware of their sameness by encountering difference, is their social structure established by their family relations. Emanating from that is what they learn to value. When pressed to say what they thought set them apart from non-Chinese, all of my informants eventually confessed that their parents expected them to follow the standards set for them in their homes. Very early in their lives, Chinese children are taught that there exists a large distance between right and wrong. In the extreme, on mainland China, being "right" at all times is the only way a child can "expect any warmth and affection from his family. Whenever he makes mistakes he will be disciplined by authority; and the essence of Chinese discipline in the home is a ruthless use of shame. The child is made to feel the humiliation of his errors and to believe that whenever he fails in meeting the appropriate standards of behavior others will look down on him," (Pye 1992:95).

"All non-Chinese think we're really smart," a high school girl said to me one day during a break in class. Several other girls and one middle school boy sitting near us agreed.

"But the truth is, we just have to study hard," Ching, the boy, added. "When we were in Taiwan, we would sometimes have to stay up very late studying. My older brother and sister had tutors; and they would work many nights until 11 o'clock."

Another girl—the young lady who I helped with her art history presentation of Kollwitz and O'Keefe and to whom I described the Rothko chapel—told me about her little sister (age seven years) who was made to go without lunch one day before her Evergreen class. "My mom and dad are really angry at her today," Elaine told me. "They don't think she's studying hard enough and learning to speak Chinese well enough. She didn't finish her homework before class today, and they wouldn't let her eat lunch even though she cried that she was really hungry. 'If you don't have time to do your homework, you don't have time to eat!' " Elaine related to me her parents' harsh judgment on her little sister. A few weeks later, I asked Elaine about her sister's progress at Evergreen and was told the little girl was applying herself. She replied in the positive, adding, "She's learning discipline!"

An intense emphasis on scholastic achievement among Chinese immigrating here not only sets them apart from the earlier coolies but it is also clearly the vehicle for upward mobility. The image of Chinese immigrants has greatly improved in recent years, in part because by 1980, they had become the best-educated group in the United States (Pan:277-278). The Chinese are represented in the media as super-achievers, as a success story of the American Dream. And this accolade has not gone unnoticed by non-Chinese of this country. We're told that many "at Stanford University will have heard the story of the white American engineering student who, told by his professor that he could have done better in his exams, retorted, 'What do you think I am, Chinese?'. . .To counter the stereotype of Chinese as narrow engineering prodigies, first-year students have been known to wear buttons proclaiming I AM NOT A CHINESE AMERICAN ELECTRICAL ENGINEER," (Pan:278).

The success achieved by so many Asian immigrants to this country is stereotypically translated by the moniker "model minority," (cf. Klineberg:11-12). It is not surprising to me that none of my informants ever referred to themselves in this manner, because inculturated humility and good *li* are highly esteemed among the Chinese, particularly among those in my study group. Yet the "model minority" stereotype persists in its application to the Asian community. "This widely held image is based on the assumption that Asians arrived in the country with little money and few skills and that they succeeded solely by virtue of hard work, high intelligence, and strong vales. Hence, at least by implication, Houston's Blacks and Hispanics have only themselves to blame if they have not achieved equal success," (ibid.:11). In Harris County (which the 1990 U.S. census indicates has more than 25,000 of the total Chinese in this metroplex area), Klineberg's study reports that 90 percent of all Asian adults are first-generation immigrants (He groups those from China, Hong Kong, and Taiwan indistinctive of their percentiles but indicates their group comprises 25 percent of all Asians in Houston.) (ibid.:6 and 11). His data, however, indicates that the "model minority" has been relatively successful in Houston primarily because the Asians "come from families in their countries of origin whose educational and occupational attainments far exceed the average for native-born Americans. When asked what occupation their fathers had when they themselves were 16 years old [sic], 36 percent of Houston's Asian population said their fathers were doctors, lawyers, professors, engineers, corporate managers, or other professionals. This was true of just 28 percent of Anglos, 19 percent of Blacks, and 13 percent of Hispanics.

"The Asians were also less likely than any other group to have been raised in the homes of production workers, farmers, or unskilled laborers. Only 20 percent of Asians said that their fathers were in such lower-status occupations, compared to 46 percent of Anglos, 60 percent of Blacks, and 67 percent of Hispanics.

"The surveys show that there has actually been *more* upward mobility from one generation to the next among Houston's Anglos, Blacks, and Hispanics than in the Asian community itself,"

(Klineberg:11). Conclusively, the "model minority" stereotype overlooks the elite class advantages of the Asian immigrants in their countries of origin and creates another kind of discrimination which feeds on the assumption that all Asians are prosperous and thus makes it less likely that those in need will be given the help that others receive (cf. Klineberg 12-13).

Of course, the large numbers of Asians immigrating to Houston (as well as to the rest of the country) do so under widely divergent circumstances such as a search for freedom, economic opportunity, political persecution, geographic and climatic catastrophe, and as a result of war. The older adult Chinese in my study group stated that they came for higher education. The younger adults came for economic opportunities; but they told me they were just as highly concerned about the educational opportunities for their children.

There are a large number of private schools in Houston, and some of them have particularly fine reputations for academic achievement. One of the most prominent is St. John's, and I talked with several different Chinese family members whose children were either presently attending the school or had graduated from there within the previous five years. Several of these parents are very active participants in the school's development programs, and one of these is on the board of directors. One day during a conversation about educational opportunities in Houston, one of these mothers mentioned that St. John's wanted "to recruit minority students." I wondered what she meant by "minority," and she clarified that as "Asian" students, although her speech context really was "Chinese" students. She said she thought this move by the school was intended to raise the academic rating there. It was unclear by her speech at that time whether she was asserting that Chinese are smarter than "American" students, but I know this mother well enough to say that she does not privilege the Chinese intelligence over the "Americans," but she does emphasize hard work and dedication with her children.

Did "being smart" ever occur to the Chinese, individually or collectively? My observation of the Chinese is that they never accept individual accolades; but they always defer to the collective achievement and anticipated fulfillment of obligation. An example is a renowned local Chinese engineer who upon being congratulated for a particular scientific discovery immediately attributed his honor to the teamwork of his 20-plus associates and deflected all individual praise from himself.

"We all worked together," I heard him say repeatedly. "I did not do this by myself. I had a dream one night that the formula should be thus (and he explained what his dream had revealed); the next day and daily for two weeks after that, my team worked to prove my dream. I was wrong. But they never questioned me. They all worked together with me to see if what I dreamed was right. It wasn't. We gave up after those two weeks and tried another approach—together." It was obvious that this well-known scientist didn't want anyone—Chinese or not—to give him sole credit for what he believed he did with other's help.

Besides working for research institutions or universities or the Taipei Economic and Cultural Office (the name for what would otherwise be the Taiwan consul if the United States had diplomatic relations with the Taiwanese government), some of my informants own their own businesses and still others work for large corporations. One of my informants, visibly distressed, talked to me one day about his unhappiness working in one such large corporation. He is one of the few Chinese working in his branch office, and his position there has a huge emphasis on management as well as on customer relations. He may come into contact with as many as one hundred customers each day, most of them non-Chinese.

"Every few months when it is time for my boss to evaluate my performance, I get the highest marks in every category. Except 'creativity.' This happens EVERY TIME," he emphasized.

This man was very frustrated; he was desirous of approval from his supervisor, but he was anxious in his inability to understand what this boss meant by "being creative" or "having creativity." The greater application of this "problem" was that he was being denied several promotions in which he was convinced he would excel.

"There was no emphasis on that (creativity) when I attended the university in Taiwan. I don't know how to think that way. It's only since I've come here (to the States), and particularly since I began talking to you a few months ago about identity and differences between my Chinese culture and the West that I began to see how differently I'm judged here."

"Do you feel comfortable enough to go to your boss and say, 'I would like to address this issue of creativity on which you have evaluated me so poorly?' Can you say, 'I never was trained to think in the independent way you expect from me? Can we discuss this issue, and perhaps reach a better understanding about how you would like me to perform my work here?'" I asked.

Reluctantly, he replied, "Oh, maybe."

When I talked to my acquaintance again a month later, I asked him whether he had ever tried to approach his supervisor about the creativity issue.

"I'm giving my notice on Monday," he told me. "I don't know if my boss will take me seriously. Out of frustration, I've given my notice two times previously, although I never went through with leaving. But now I've found another opportunity that is going to give me more money, more responsibility, and a challenge to make the business grow."

"Now there's a creative resolution/solution!" I thought. It seems the obvious difference between my acquaintance and his boss was the stereotypical issue of lack of communication.

Thinking "creatively" in Western society is often inseparably linked to thinking independently. In traditional Chinese thought and expression in one's life, to act independently is not only an anomaly; it is tantamount to invalidating the systems which inform one's identity (cf. Wang, L.; cf. Liang Qichao). A Chinese student at Columbia University in the 1930s, reflecting on the American model, wrote, " 'Individualism,' it should be noted, is a word that in Chinese connotes a degree of selfishness. That America is a most extremely individualistic nation can be seen from the family system and family life; that material civilization there is highly developed is apparent in family life; and that this is the most pleasure-seeking nation in the world at present is likewise something that can be seen in family life. . . *Individualism* means, first that people all look after themselves and are not dependent on others. Second, it means that all have the right to determine their own actions, and that, except after due process of law, no one may interfere with these—neither the government with its citizens, nor a group with its members, nor parents with their children, nor a husband with his wife. . .The other aspect of individualism is that

'Every man is his own boss' and no one may interfere with another. There is a common American expression, 'Mind your own business', which at first glance seems to mean the same thing as the Chinese saying, 'Each sweeps the snow from before his own door; none cares about the frost on another's roof.' But the former implies 'you stay out of my business,' which expresses the desire to avoid the trouble or complications of involvement in others' affairs," ("Gongwang" in Arkush and Lee 1989:146).

Another concern over the us-them dichotomy is a financial trait: frugality *(jian)*.[1] But I had not been aware that it was an issue about which they felt so protective until one day an Evergreen mother asked me, "Did you see the newspaper this morning? A Chinese man from Hong Kong gave $100 million to Princeton. I'm glad that's in the paper. Now the world won't think we're always so stingy!"

I've come to see now that this frugality is part of the identity among my study group, and some of them apparently care that this trait may stand in obvious disparity to the free-spending Western consumerism and apparent disregard for avidly saving. On one occasion, a younger informant explained that she had to do her homework right after school, because she was expected to work in her uncle's restaurant. Her comment reminded me that many times I had seen young people (They looked to be high school age.) serve and clean up in what were apparently family-owned and -run businesses in Chinatown. After one such experience, I commented to an informant that the Chinese food I ate near the Strake Jesuit campus was so delicious, so flavorful, so fresh-tasting. And it was so very different from the "generic" Chinese restaurants outside of Chinatown. I thought it was noteworthy, too, that this savory meal was so cheap! Not inexpensive. *Cheap.*

"That's about right," she responded when calculating what the bill should be. "Everybody old enough in the family works together. Labor is nothing. The rent is low, and the food costs are low, because they buy everything fresh—not packaged."

" 'Labor is nothing?!' " I kept this thought to myself wondering whether this was a Chinese perspective on the value of one's contribution to a group effort. More likely, in the scheme of things, labor is not an economic factor here; it is a family responsibility—literally a means of serving one another.

A few weeks later when talking with a Rice University student about Chinese identity, particularly about how she regarded herself as an ethnic Chinese in Houston and those family values which influenced her life here, she emphasized education and why her parents are glad she is attending Rice. "Be sure and put this in your dissertation: write about frugality!" she encouraged me. "My parents read those reports in *Fortune* magazine. Rice is absolutely the best academic value. That's it! The Chinese are *so* concerned with getting a good education, and they are *so* concerned about not spending a lot of money!"

I related to her my conversation with a Chinese woman about the restaurant pricing system and her comments particularly that "labor is nothing."

"Your interpretation is right," she said in support. "It's not that we don't value the effort of our family members; we all have obligations we are expected to perform, and we're not always consciously congratulating each other on our contributions."

NOTES

1. Parenthetical to this is the Chinese pride in money management. No Chinese was on relief during the Depression of the 1930s (Chen and von der Mehden:4).

X

The Evergreen Youth Club

It was their idea. Several of the high school kids decided they wanted to have an extra curriculum activity among themselves at Evergreen, and more than 50 students, the principal, and several of the teachers (who were also parents of some of the students) attended the first meeting. One of the organizers, an extremely vivacious and mature freshman girl named Janie from my classroom, asked me to attend, too, as an honored guest.

"And will you be our sponsor?" she asked.

"Oh! Well, yes!" I responded, extremely flattered. (An older Chinese friend whose children had attended Evergreen many years before later commented to me about being asked to be part of their group, "That's good. You're one of them. They like you!" I later remembered that it was Janie who had led the applause in class the day I was asked to speak extemporaneously on racism and ended my "speech" by encouraging them to learn more about their culture and language so they could create an understanding of Chinese for non-Chinese people.)

So the meeting commenced in what I expected to be a perfunctory introduction by the principal, but she quickly established an exclusionary rule of the after-school activity: no one who was not a student of Evergreen could be part of the club. Right away, approximately 20 students had to withdraw from the meeting. They were all Chinese, (many of them had attended Evergreen before but were now attending other well-thought of Chinese language schools), and they had been invited by the same girl from Jack's class who had invited me. The principle continued speaking with a very decisive tone in her voice that told us she had firmly made up her mind on the subject of membership.

"I'm really sorry, guys," Janie told them. "I thought you could be part of our group, too." Aside, she quietly said to me that the principle had told her she *could* invite all the non-Evergreen students who were walking out the door but had changed her mind without telling Janie. The reasoning for exclusionary membership was that opening the doors to outsiders might be an invitation to "unacceptable" membership (i.e., local Vietnamese gangs who were known trouble-makers). Janie was embarrassed for the inconvenience her friends were caused, but she didn't dwell on the event and instead continued to conduct the remainder of the meeting with Bob who was a high school senior at the time and also a member of Jack's class.

"We're here for two purposes," they jointly told all of us in the room. "First, we want to develop leadership qualities; and secondly, we're going to have activities that will be a contribution to the community."

I sat on the side of the room next to Joyce and her distant cousin, and I wondered silently whether "community" was going to be defined. Just when I fully expected the meaning to be the "Chinese community," Bob and Janie proposed events such as soup kitchens at Thanksgiving and clothing drives for the poor. Then they proposed that the club visit "elders homes" (homes for the retired, impaired, or indigent). Unmistakably, they were talking about non-Chinese, greater-Houston activities that would foster better relations and give the club the status of being concerned about others beyond the Chinese community.

"There will be certificates awarded for your participation," the principal injected as my two classmates stood at the front of the room addressing the others.

"Will this count toward being a National Merit Scholar?" came a voice from the back of the room.

"Yeah, and can we get credit for this at our regular high school?" another asked.

A discussion of the proposed activities ensued, including various means of fund raising which would also provide a fun social time, such as a Christmas dance or a car wash. Then, for me, who repeatedly had read and was told by "traditional" Chinese parents that "individualism is a bad thing in Chinese culture," a bombshell was dropped:

"We want you all to be thinking about electing officers for this club," Bob announced. "Very soon we'll need to have a president, a vice-president, a secretary-historian, and a treasurer. Please don't just vote for the people you know, because you haven't gotten to know everyone here yet. Whoever wants to run for office must come up before us and tell the club members his or her qualifications; each person must tell why he or she is the best person for the job. We need to vote according to who we think will be the best and not just vote for our friends."

Janie added, "Just jump up, tells us your name, and tell us why you want to be and should be that officer."

Everyone in the room seemed to accept this as rather normal (although I later realized there was a division between the ABCs and the immigrants), but *I* was floored!! For more than a year, I had been told many times by older (35-years-plus) Chinese men and women—from Hong Kong, mainland China, and from Taiwan—that one is taught in Chinese culture *never* to talk about oneself in a manner that could be interpreted by the listener as braggadocios. "If one is told that he or she has done a good job, one must reply, 'Oh no, it's not very good.' And if someone asks, 'Do you know how to do this?' you must reply, 'No, I can't do that,' and then you go ahead and do it to the best of your ability." So many times I was told, "One has to be humble and not act so worthy."

A few days later I telephoned Jack (who had not been present at that first meeting of the club) and described to him the club officer election scenario. Jack, who is in his early 40s and was born and raised in Taiwan, agreed with my other older informants that being humble was *de rigueur* decorum in Chinese society.

"That's true," was his response to my understanding that the students exemplified a new standard of Chinese behavior. "But I tell the students, 'That (way of showing humility) is the old way. This is today. You have to stand up for yourself. You have to speak up. You can't be shy. Show the world who you are.' The older students who have older parents, like Bob, have been raised in a very traditional household. But many of them have acquired modern, liberal ideas about how to act and think about themselves."

This is a curious situation for the students at Evergreen and particularly for those in the youth club. All of these kids have parents born on mainland China or Taiwan and raised and schooled on the island under the aegis of the Nationalists. Expectedly, not only have their parents not abandoned their attitudes of social behavior which they acquired when they were very young, they have applied these values to raising these same kids who attend Evergreen. Without exception and in the dutiful fashion in which they are being raised, the high school seniors who talk about the colleges they would like to attend speak with resignation that they just aren't good enough students. They often say "I'd like to go (to here or to there)," and they each always finish their sentences with, "Oh, but I'm sure I can't get in."

Bob, for example, tells me that at home his father says to him that Bob is wasting his time applying to some schools (such as the University of California at Berkeley because, "The competition is too great for Asians; and besides, it's too liberal." Bob also has applied to Stanford and to Rice where he wants to major in engineering.) Bob, however, is an outstanding student in academics as well as in his extracurricular music activities; he's also quite fluent in Chinese and often scores very highly on the Evergreen exams.

These Evergreen students have accommodated themselves to bicultural thinking that does not fuse their traditional Chinese attitudes of subordinating the individual to authority with highly stylized Western individualism. Rather, these kids are living a kind of para-culture in the sense that the home culture/attitudes are alongside the Western education/social experiences. Given the situation, these kids appropriate behavior and attitudes which *they* think are fitting. In conversation they always refer to their parents with respect for their authority. But I've also observed that when the parents are present among the kids' friends, such as at the youth club meetings, rather than abjure their "Western" individualistic behavior, they merely modify their outspokenness to a more "measured" expression.

The club's first significant community contribution was to serve Thanksgiving dinner to the less fortunate in Houston. The Wednesday before Thanksgiving the first year of the club, the kids assembled at the parking lot of Strake Jesuit, and those with cars and those whose parents agreed to carpool rode downtown to the George R. Brown convention center.[1]

"This makes me feel so good to be doing something for someone else," Janie told me the weekend before. We're going to be putting on toques and aprons and serving and cleaning. I'm just so happy about this! I'm glad to help someone else. And I'm glad that people will see us Chinese making a contribution to Houston's needy, too."

NOTES

1. I refer the reader to page 39 on which I described the convention center and its significant position/relationship to the older, downtown Chinatown.

XI

Parents Trying to Raise Chinese Kids
in the West

"It's so hard to raise our children here the way my parents raised me. It's so hard to keep our language," a mother lamented one afternoon after school.

Her oldest daughter was born in Houston, but the family lived a lengthy time in Hong Kong before returning to Houston. Her concern about extending her children's Chinese cultural identity beyond the home is so great that she volunteers to teach a language class at Evergreen. She and her husband also insist that their children participate in programs such as the summer Chinese camp in Huntsville, which brings together 350 Chinese youth mostly from the Houston area for a week each July since 1985 to speak Chinese and have a collective experience making friends and playing games (Huntsville is located 80 miles north, northwest of Houston enroute to Dallas which is 240 miles from Houston.). When their children are college-age, they will attend the same Summer Language Training Program in Taipei that Jimmy and his sister attended.

"The distance from home (Taiwan) is very difficult for me, too. My parents are old, and I am very concerned about taking care of them. I am here, and they are there, (cf. Chang:200)."

This dual leitmotif of 1) distance which doesn't sever duty to one's parents and 2) a desire for their children to keep their Chinese language and some semblance of Chinese traditions was part of every parent's conversation with me. They took for granted that everyday their kids encountered non-Chinese attitudes toward family obligations and examples of permissive individualism. Yet their knowledge of (and in many cases, projection of) their children's lives beyond their home environment, was countered with strong messages of filial obligation.

I asked Larry one day whether his family talks about what kind of friends he has or who he goes out with. "No, they don't tell me who my friends can be. And I don't go out. At night at dinner they talk about family. They talk about opportunities they want us to have. It is our responsibility to do our best to deserve those opportunities," was his reply.

On another afternoon I visited a smaller classroom where the teacher was asking the students to translate "depend on." "How many of you have heard your parents say this," she asked: "'I worked hard and didn't win the Nobel Prize. I'm depending on *you* to win it!'"

Forty percent of the students in the room raised their hands! Of course, they knew she was being facetious using the Nobel Prize as the object, that her intention was to exemplify a much-admired achievement.

I found divisiveness by gender when the subject of high school dating or socializing after school and on weekends came up. "Do any of the high school girls date?" I asked an uncounted number of female students from Taiwan.

"No," they all said. But one pointed to Janie and said that she had a date with a Chinese boy to go to the high school prom.

"We can go to parties at our friends' houses if their parents are there," another said. There are (Chinese) boys and other (Chinese) girls there."

I extended this inquiry to a journalist for a Chinese newspaper whose comments included community attitudes of intermarriage and gender as well as his attitudes toward his own daughter's social life. "It depends on your background," he answered. "Traditional Chinese are against intermarriage. But immigrants (here) are open-minded. If they weren't open-minded they wouldn't move here; they would move to Japan, another Asian country. Families are more protective of girls because of the social problems in the greater Houston (and Western) society, (cf. Chang:63-69)." He continued mentioning the "social problems" and specifically mentioned rape and other "social ills to which girls are more vulnerable and less successful to defend themselves from attack."

"Why do you think Chinese girls are not allowed to date?" I asked Joyce.

Her matter-of-fact reply startled me: "Girls are more likely to give themselves (their affections) to boys. Having sex with a boy would bring shame to the family."

"Having sex outside of marriage is considered immoral?" an almost needless (I thought) question.

"No. It has nothing to do with morals. It's because if a girl got pregnant, that pregnancy would bring shame to the family. There's not the same responsibility put on boys, because they can't get pregnant."

"Would you consider marrying a non-Chinese girl?" I asked a university senior active in his Chinese student association.

"No, never," was his reply. "The Chinese born outside of the United States put a lot of pressure on the ABCs within our student association who date non-Chinese. Even other Asians are off-limits to these people who so strongly try to influence the ABCs to date only other Chinese."

A mother of a son and a daughter told me of her sadness that her daughter (an ABC) is in graduate school and still doesn't date Chinese boys. In fact, this young woman is having a several-years-old romance with a white man who followed her from her Ivy League school where they graduated together with undergraduate degrees to the mid-western town in which she now lives and studies. The father of this young woman shook his head in conversation with me and lamented that despite his and his wife's attempts to influence her differently, despite their raising her in a home where Chinese was always spoken and Chinese traditions were always revered, she has always had mostly non-Chinese friends and only non-Chinese boyfriends. This young woman is known among Chinese and non-Chinese alike to be very strong-willed and independently-minded. The son, by contrast, is more compliant. I came to know him as an informant, and I brought up the issue of intermarriage one day in conversation. It never occurred to him not to marry a Chinese woman, it seemed. Over a period of time that we would converse, his sensitivity to the marriage issue intensified. To the delight of his parents (who related this to me), the younger brother recently told his sister that he intends to marry only a Chinese girl and, consequently, is no longer even considering dating anyone except Chinese. "I'm so glad he told her that!" the mother smiled some days later. "I know she (the daughter) was startled. There's still time (for her to find a Chinese boyfriend)!"

Another adult informant whose three children were born here (two of whom are now grown and living away from Houston) offered another story of Chinese parents who often feel upset and lacking authority in the lives of their ABC children. It seems that two years earlier, a 13-year-old boy ran away from home. He was found by his parents, but the high school counselor for the boy (a non-Chinese person) said to the parents that they should just let the boy (now 15-years-old) stay away until he feels like coming home. Understandably, the parents are terribly distraught: they want to respond to their son's plight, and they recognize the Western influence which was so instrumental in his leaving; yet they want to raise him in a Chinese family environment. At the time of this writing, the issue, sadly, is still unresolved.

At another juncture at Evergreen I wondered out loud within a group whether the kids had been taught civic pride by their parents. "Do you have a responsibility to be instrumental in your culture?" I asked the group collectively.

"Yes, because the world doesn't know enough about Chinese culture; we must be able to tell the world more about us," only one girl out of a dozen students answered. I remained curious that there were no more responses than one out of twelve (even though I had known these kids almost a year when I first posed this question). But I have since decided that an absence of more answers was not due to their reluctance to talk to me; in their daily experience of living in Houston, they simply think they are part of Houston and, ergo, making a contribution indistinctive of their total effort to fulfill their daily responsibilities. Their lives here are lived as complete Chinese living in Houston. They, especially at their young ages, see no contradiction to this anymore than if someone were to suggest to them that they would be *more complete* or *more exemplary* Chinese if they were living in Taipei, or Beijing, or Singapore, or Shanghai, etc.

I addressed the next question to everyone in the room but, in particular, to this young lady who had just answered me: "What is essential about being Chinese?"

"It's to keep the family values and bring honor to the family," she replied. "We study all the time in our social studies classes that we Chinese have family values, and the West has no family values. We must keep this honor to our families."

"You read that in your social studies class?!"

"Yes. In Taiwan."

I consciously kept a moderated tone, but I wanted to shriek. Calmly, I asked, "You are told that Westerners have no family values?"

"Well, the government twists everything there."

Was it really the "government" twisting things, I wondered sarcastically to myself, or was this indicative of xenophobic culture perpetuated by the family unit? I dismissed the attitude that as a Westerner I had "no family values," regained some mental composure, and asked a number of Evergreen parents about their daunting task of raising their children: "What were they doing; what were they expecting from their children; and what did they think of the results so far?"

"You know, Ai Lien (my Chinese name which my informants gave me early on in my fieldwork), we say of ourselves that we are in the middle. We want to serve our parents, and we want to serve our children." This was a mother whose two children had attended Evergreen when it was still located on the Rice University campus. I had gotten to know Sylvia well during the course of my "being in the field," and dropped by her house one morning to chat. Her comments of "we are in the middle" were a response to my comment that it must be difficult for her to raise her children here (in the States) with a strong sense of Chinese tradition and identity, all the while trying to remain devoted to her parents. For example, I was keenly aware that even though Sylvia is nearly 50-years-old, she still telephones her mother in Taipei when Sylvia is uncertain about the "right way" to behave in a social situation. An example is the time several months earlier that Sylvia had purchased non-refundable airline tickets for a short holiday for herself and her husband. A few weeks before they were to leave for their trip, Sylvia learned that a cousin's child was being married in New

York, and Sylvia was invited to the large wedding. I remember her saying to me at the time, "Ai Lien, I don't know what to do." Then, as if speaking to herself, she turned to talk to the space in the room and said, "I'll have to call my mother and ask her what I should do."

Admittedly, I offered her my advice. I thought she should telephone her cousin (with whom, after all, she wasn't very close), explain that she had already made some plans that involved others, send a nice gift to the cousin's child that she had not seen since he was five-years-old, and go to her vacation spot.

Sylvia's mother told her to go to the wedding. So, she went to the wedding. (Sylvia's husband couldn't have cared less. He took his golf clubs to the wedding that weekend and played with the cousin's husband whenever the two of them could find a lull in the social activities.)

I really wasn't so surprised at the choice Sylvia made. Numerous times I heard Chinese speak about the important roles their parents and their in-laws played in these people's lives. One evening during the Chinese New Year festivities, I was delighted to be invited to some informants' home for a large celebratory dinner. Positions around the table were arranged to honor the various guests; and I was very interested to see that by standards of Chinese decorum, the most venerable were seated opposite one another in the middle of the longest part of a rectilinear arrangement. In this case, the two most honored couples out of 30 people were a retired mathematics professor who at the urging of Albert Einstein, had been smuggled by the U. S. government out of China with his family in 1949, and a high-ranking ambassador for the Taiwanese government. I was seated near the corner of the table (which didn't seem so bad because the host sat to the right of me, and he had an accentuated flex to his wrist whenever he poured the wine), and the diplomat's daughter, Lucy, sat to my left.

Never having been to such a gathering, I was intrigued that guests were selectively placed here and there in an obvious pattern which placed male children closest to their parents, female children next to the honored guest who was *not* her parent, and the in-laws and non-family guests to the outside. When Lucy learned of my interest in Chinese culture, particularly how that culture translates to the West, she began a near-monologue about Chinese history and customs. To her, an explanation of living Chinese culture outside of China was not a matter of translation; the Chinese were the same everywhere. It was the non-Chinese who needed to adjust to an understanding of the Chinese around them.

"In our culture, family is the most important thing. We all live together. I live with my husband and our children, and with his brother, his brother's wife, and their children; and we all live together with my in-laws," Lucy explained. "We all work together. My sister-in-law does most of the cooking, and I carpool the children to school and other activities," (cf. Chang:182).

"A bit too cozy for me," I thought. I also thought that was a rather simplified version of older feudal times. Even later, I related this conversation with Lucy to the hostess and said, "That's not Chinese; that's the in-laws' *control!*" Still, I appreciated Lucy's insight. I became quietly amused when she began a history lesson, emphasizing the period of the struggle for the Republic and making a crescendo with the triumphant establishment of the KMT in Taiwan and the subsequent "democratic" and economic glories now reigning in Taiwan.

Lucy's position as the daughter of a man prominent in promulgating the best of what Taiwan has to offer—and procuring for Taiwan the best the world has to offer—certainly locates her outside the sphere of normal Chinese lives. "The quintessential diplomatic family influence," I thought. Then, while trying to digest Lucy's loyalist bent, I recalled the root word of diplomat comes from the Greek word for "double!"

Sometime later, an acquaintance of Lucy whose children attend the same private school with Lucy's children, sat very pensively for a few minutes after I asked her, "What are you expecting from your children in this predominantly non-Chinese West, and what do you think of the results so far?"

"You know, I'm not so sure it's so bad to be a 'banana.' My kids speak Chinese and visit often with their grandparents who were born, raised, and educated on mainland China. But I want my kids to be American. I want them to get an education here and be proud that they're living in freedom in this country.

"I don't know what's next for these kids in Chinese schools like Evergreen, though," she added. "They really don't speak Chinese that well, even in the highest classes." (She added an explanation that since the kids don't speak Chinese all the time, and since they live in an Otherwise community during their waking hours—at school, at the mall, involved mostly in non-Chinese entertainment activities—the result is they don't understand the same nuances of their language in the same way as their traditionally-reared parents.) "But then, they really don't need to speak Chinese to have a Chinese school."

In the several times I spoke with this mother, never did she refer to her own children nor to other Chinese children here in a hyphenated manner. Rather, she would often switch in conversation from a reference to the kids as Chinese to a reference to them as American (the ABCs in particular). Living here and raising children here was not a contradiction to her cultural sensibilities. Nor was it a case of assimilating a reference to a ChineseAmerican (a word I've purposefully written as a statement of unity). Instead, I saw this woman's expression as a commentary among the discourse I so often encountered in the Houston/Evergreen Chinese community: rather than serve as hybrids or America's newest ingredients to the melting pot, these people intend to live here as a paracommunity. That is, they live beside and with the non-Chinese; but in their minds they remain set apart.

Beyond the home when the kids are with their classmates at school or even away at college, there's a temptation that exists for any young person to resist their parents' guidelines and indulge in more independent behavior. For many Chinese, rather than deny their Chinese identity or disregard so many of the standards by which they were raised, they seek to join Chinese student associations. "So even if they say they don't want to go to Chinese school when they're younger," a parent told me, "when they go away to college they take Chinese courses and join a student association."

"Some Chinese say they don't need to join such a club or association," a college student told me. "But for me, especially since I grew up in the southwestern part of the United States where there were a lot of Hispanics and fewer Chinese, it's refreshing to know there are *a lot* of people like me. I joined the Chinese student association (at my university) because it's like a network that allows us an opportunity to explore our culture.

"When my brother and I were growing up, our parents made sure we spoke Chinese, that we understood how important it was to get a good education, that we respected our parents, and that we worked hard. My mother, in particular, was really hard on us about our grades. I remember so well that she used to slap the palms of our open hands—I mean really hit them hard—when we had deficient grades. One hit was given for each grade below a perfect 100 (e.g., A score of 95 was punished with five hard slaps on the open hand.)."

"Why?!" I was amazed that such a good grade could be a punishable offense.

"Because that was the standard enforced on her when she was in school in Taiwan. That's the way she was raised, so that is what she thought she had to do to us, even though we lived in New Mexico!"

Conclusion

XII

Are You a Different Chinese in Houston?

A friend of mine was born in the early 1920s to parents who had migrated to Virginia from England only a few years earlier. These parents were well-spoken and not only held on to their distinctive accent that spoke to their upper-class education but also insisted that their son always speak the mother tongue clearly and elegantly (My friend later became an Anglican priest known for his resonant voice and brilliant oratorical skills from the pulpit!). As he was growing up in Virginia, of course he learned that he was living in an historically significant part of the country. His grandmother came from England to live with the family while my friend was about five-years-old. One day the grandmother was in the kitchen where in those days large ovens (always warm) dominated the room. "Grandmother," my friend asked her as he came into the kitchen, "are we English?" This proud grandmother snapped back, "If the mother cat has her kittens in the oven, do we call them *biscuits*?!"

The issue of "What is essential about being Chinese?" is at the core of understanding the identity of these people. In every case I investigated at Evergreen, in every personal exchange I had with Chinese regarding what was important in their lives, regarding what was characteristic about their having a Chinese identity, the answers always included their conformity to standards exacted at the value placed on family relations and adherence to a long-standing belief in "right behavior." Their vocabulary of social conformity and resistance of self-centered aggrandizement emerges whenever there is a discussion about how they see themselves in relation to those non-

Chinese around them. It is clear that my informants intended for me to see that they shared an attitudinal sameness in the most general way. I never felt that they wanted me to forget that they were Chinese. But, of course, that was the basis of our relationship: I was there to see them as Chinese and to learn what they thought of themselves. Did they become more aware of being Chinese by my being with them and asking questions about them? I'm certain the answer is yes.

The entire Evergreen class had an amusing exchange with me one weekend when I spoke a Chinese phrase to them that at first only Jack recognized. *"Ni chi le ma?"* ("Have you eaten?") I asked. This traditional greeting used among Chinese helps to illustrate a portrait of a people who Belle Yang describes as being "intensely preoccupied with the state of the stomach—more so, I am prone to believe, than any other fold to inhabit this earth," (Yang:3). There is no intention of inviting to dinner the person being greeted ("nor does the one thus greeted harbor any illusion of having been invited") (ibid.). The phrase is simply a means of asking, "How are you?" I suppose one might go further to explain this as a means of fellowship, of asking if one is doing well, of asking whether one is prosperous (i.e., eating well), as a means of showing concern, etc. The anticipated response is *"Chi guo le, chi guo le,"* "Yes, yes, I've eaten," (a repetitive means of substantiating one is doing well).[1]

"What?" several of the kids around me responded.

"Don't you speak Chinese?" I teased them. Many were the times my informants good-naturedly corrected my Mandarin pronunciations. But this time I was certain I was speaking correctly. The problem was they were unfamiliar with the greeting. I went to some length explaining the significance of this greeting in traditional Chinese culture, and only after several minutes did some of the kids recall that their parents would use the phrase with their parents' friends. Even Jack said he used to hear and speak the greeting; but since being in Houston for several years, its use "seemed to be less and less likely."

I asked Larry if the greeting were used in South Africa; and he, also, was unfamiliar with it. "Oh, you know what it means," Jack teased him. He (wearing a black leather jacket) aggressively approached Larry and said, "It's a greeting like the Mafia coming up to you and saying, 'Are you still alive?!' "

What amused me about this exchange is that it underlined a modest change between the customs of the China of their past and their present life. Certainly the difference in phraseology was not generational but rather environmental; as preoccupied with food as some writers often characterize the Chinese, the speech conceptions continue to undergo alteration for the Chinese who are living bi-culturally in Houston. Only a few months before when I had run across the phrase in my research, I brought it up with a Chinese acquaintance who often laughs a "confession" of her bi-monthly four-hour lunches with her friends. "You know, I seldom hear it these days. And when I do, I sometimes forget what it means; and I say, 'No, thank you.' I've been here so long (25 years). Some of these things are different for me now," she explained.

One day on another occasion when Sylvia and I were visiting, the subject of my daughter's recent birthday party came up. Sylvia commented to me about never having celebrated her children's birthdays. Jenny, her oldest who was born in the States, has moved away; and though unmarried, she seldom makes an effort to come home for her birthday (which is December 21) and the holiday season. Her mother prays at the Buddhist temple and thus has no religious sensitivity to Christmas nor to the holiday season. Sylvia told me that her daughter occasionally gets unhappy with her that she grew up with school friends (Westerners) who had birthday celebrations and yet Jenny only had one party her whole adolescent life. "But Ai Lien, when I was growing up I never had a birthday party either. In traditional Chinese the parents don't give their children parties. When the children are grown, they are supposed to give their *parents* the parties; when a child is little, there is no celebrating the day the mother suffered. I guess now that I think about it, I better tell Jenny that. I never told her before. I just thought she understood that."

"It's important not to think of the Chinese as a monolithic thing," a Chinese educator stressed to me. He wanted to be certain that I did not have a narrow interpretation of us-them camps. Rather, he was proud of his heritage and the scholarly investigation which had revealed more to him about the land of his birth (mainland China). Still, he described himself as "a marginal man with both cultures. I'm not acculturated into being just Chinese anymore. You're neither Chinese nor Western after living in this culture for awhile. Besides, I have no reason to think I'm removed from China: on any day I can go to Chinatown and pick up any number of (Chinese language) newspapers. I live and work here, but I can go back and forth between Houston and Beijing to see my family."

It seemed to me that he thought he could go back and forth between the cultures, as well, without even leaving here.

Literature is replete with retelling the lives of people who have emigrated around the world; stories of Chinese are particularly well-known not only for the massive exoduses they've sometimes made but also for the minimal standards for which they would often settle in the new lands and the diligent efforts they made to survive and succeed as new residents (cf. Yang; cf. Pan 1994; cf. McCunn 1988; cf. Kingston 1989; cf. *New York Times* 1995). Rey Chow reminds us that Chinese history has been a series of catastrophes for the past century and a half, and further says that the Tiananmen Massacre of June 4, 1989 "brought modern Chinese history to a standstill," (Chow 1993:74; cf. Kristoff and WuDunn 1994). "This is the standstill of catastrophe. . .[the events] marked their summation in the form of a mindlessly internalized violence directed against civilians by a government which barely forty years ago had stood for hope and emancipation from the corruption of the Chinese tradition," (Chow:74).

The trauma that she says continues to haunt the Chinese intellectuals has continued to galvanize the "ordinary" Chinese for some time with the question of the continuity and (re)production of culture. "This is a question about pedagogy. What can be taught to the younger generation? How is culture—in ruins—to be passed on, by whom, and with what means?" (ibid.).

Throughout the period since the early nineteenth century, which has been a time of particular ideological, political, intellectual, and emotional tumult for the Chinese, a principal structural element of Chinese culture has remained: an adherence to connection through a network of social and economic relationships (*guanxi*). This context of connection allows the contemporary Chinese to make the transition away from a traditional orientation to authority and adopt a more instrumental or situational position. The observances I made of the kids' modified para-behavior, particularly when their parents were present is such an example. But this move does not occur without consciously encountering the Other of non-Chinese culture.

How does migration affect the identity of the immigrant? And how does the immigrant affect the identity of his or her new community? Breslin, in his biography of Rothko (*ne* Marcus Rothkowitz), asks these same questions but substitutes "affect" with "threaten." Certainly these two different words provide insight into the kind of answers the two authors (he and I) are expecting. For Breslin's part, we can apply the consideration Naficy describes as liminars, "exiles [who] face two types of immanent and imminent threats simultaneously: the threat of the disappearance of the homeland and the threat of themselves disappearing in the host society," (Naficy 1993:129). Breslin writes that the new experience in America for leftist-thinking Rothko as learning that "social and political freedoms, like economic opportunities, had their ambiguities. Portland [Oregon, where Rothko's family settled] had a reputation as a progressive city, one reason Jewish immigrants settled there; but in the late teens and early twenties, the city, like the rest of the country, was dominated by reactionary politics. Certainly, there were no pogroms; but espousing radical positions at that time in Portland was *quite* dangerous," (Breslin:39).

The Chinese in my study group do not convey a sense of being threatened (either verbally or physically) in the same way as Breslin describes Rothko's experience or as Naficy describes the exilic liminar. We know that some people (racists?) who view the Chinese self-satisfaction and achievement as contrarian (particularly in academics and financial solvency) are themselves threatened. Yet the Chinese parents in my study group do express a concern that their children retain the value of family and good *li* above all else; and that, in the extreme, is underlain by the fears of embracing Western "values" of highly individualized expression without seeming to be consequential or referential to the family structure (cf. Pye 1992:95). The earlier scathing remarks about American society by Singapore's former prime minister Lee (whose state many would not hesitate to call fascist in its reaction to contrarian behavior) are representative in the extreme of some of the older Chinese I talked with. But more precise is the acknowledgment that the younger children in particular are spending most of their waking hours among non-Chinese in schools and listening to media presentations and representations which are almost wholly non-Chinese. The parents' most apodictic means of countering this is with Chinese language schools, having the youth participate in Chinese community events, encouraging the younger Chinese to develop a network of Chinese friends, and of course, insisting that they retain the Chinese values they have exemplified for them at home.

In "A Question of Identity," James Baldwin warns against applying a common denominator to a group of people resettled (albeit temporarily) from their place of origin. Merely because these people are ostensibly all in the new location (Paris, France) for the same reason (the U.S. armed services or academic interest), the measure of sameness about them does not parallel a desire to emulate the "natives" among whom they live (Baldwin 1985:91-99). For example, the student who does not flee Paris in the face of so much that is different from home very often is one "whose adaptation to French life seems to have been most perfect, and whose studies—of French art, or the drama, the language, or the history—give him the greatest right to be here. This student has put aside chewing gum forever, he eschews the T-shirt, and the crew cut, he can only with difficulty be prevailed upon to see an American movie, and it is so patent that he is *actually* studying that his appearance at the café tables is never taken as evidence of frivolity, but only as proof of his admirable passion to study the customs of the country. One assumes that he is living as the French live—which assumption, however, is immediately challenged by the suspicion that no American *can* live as the French live, even if one could find an American who wanted to," (ibid.:96). The American in Paris is confronted with the question of his identity, Baldwin says; one does not become Parisian by virtue of a Paris address. Nor does one quit being Chinese and become something else when that person leaves his Sino-geographical place of birth.

Identity for Chinese youth immigrating to the West (no less, to Houston) emerges from the opposition of the submissive connection to the authority of networks, and the dominant American (United States) individualism which promotes private self-interest and, hence, tends to sever communal relations. Since the clan associations no longer hold the traditional importance for the Chinese with whom I did my fieldwork, I have to wonder (and even project) that what may be thought of—by Chinese and Westerners alike—as a kinship-based system in reality is and will be networking. Perhaps in the future the Chinese system may not be regarded so much as an ethnically-based system but rather as a prominent system of relationship which is based on respect and trust and honor. It is obvious that as human interaction undergoes radical alteration by people in diaspora and by the discovery and introduction of new forms of understanding and relationability, no longer are people restricting themselves to old ways of conceptualizing and expressing their identity. Reaching beyond the touchstone of historical bedrock does not sever these immigrants from the corpus of their heritage. The pentimento remains. So while the clan associations no longer figure prominently in the transition a family makes from the China of the past, other—including newer—means of networking are serving the Chinese community; examples of these are certainly the Evergreen School, the Chinese student associations on college campuses, the Chinese youth groups, the Chinese summer camps, and the professional organizations for those adults with careers among non-Chinese.

While the focus of my fieldwork was the Evergreen School—and primarily the oldest and most literate students—other members of the Houston Chinese community greatly informed my understanding of their desire to live an essential idea of Chinese identity. These people's contributions to my work were as numerous as the individuals themselves; yet above all there ran a succinct theme: *a deliberate choice* to claim a commonalty to their nascent ethnicity while fashioning their way as Chinese in America. For these people I've studied, identity is similar to Bakhtin's analysis of the novel as being in a process of restructuring. Identity cannot be repeated; with each new event, with each new zone of contact, an adjustment, a change must be made to accommodate that person or persons to whom something is happening.

It has never been my intention herein to portray this group of immigrants in my study as homogeneous among themselves, the young with their parents, nor the parents with *their* parents still behind on mainland China and Taiwan. Though they certainly share Mandarin dialect and Chinese ethnicity (with the exception of Jennifer who might have a difficult time identifying herself as Han Chinese or Taiwanese— or both)—and several share relatively the same economic and social status by means of some family members serving the Taiwanese government in various civil capacities—the younger group especially differs in their emotional distance from China.

A fascinating and insightful activity (for me) happened one day in class when Jack handed out maps of contiguous mainland China, including the Tibetan region which the communist Chinese military forcefully invaded four decades ago under pretense of ethnic and cultural kinship.[2] The provinces, known as *sheng*, were labeled in Chinese. He then wrote on the chalkboard in Chinese script the names of each of these provinces and called out to each student in the room asking them individually to quickly name their home. Although each gave an answer, I could overhear some students say in embarrassed hushed tones that they weren't sure of where they came from. What intrigued me was that, with the exception of Debbie who was born in Canton and moved to Hong Kong before coming to Houston, everyone there was born in Taiwan. Yet they are expected to think that their place of origin is actually where their ancestors lived in China.[3] I later asked Jack why he would expect these students to respond to "Where are you from?" with the answers of their ancestors' province of origin. It seemed that it simply never occurred to him that where he was *born* was not the place that he was *from*.

This sense of belonging to something else while fashioning for themselves here a new life is not only non-contradictory for the Chinese I've studied; rather, it is part of the portrait design of these immigrants to remain eclectic in their pursuit of balance and harmony. While they demonstrated a desire to me to be instrumental in the greater Houston community, the need for approval of the white majority—so common a thread in immigrant history—does not even occur to these people (cf. Pan:275-295). By contrast, Irving Howe writes of "a certain mode of apologia" among immigrants which he says "creeps into their self-considerations. They 'point with pride' to the contributions they have made to American society: writers, baseball players, musicians, night-club comedians, millionaires, radicals, physicists, politicians. Behind such apologia lies an unspoken assumption that a court of native American opinion has the right to pass final judgment, deciding whether or not immigrant cultures merit acceptance and respect," Howe:645). Referring particularly to east European Jewish immigrants, he says that while they "can claim an abundant share of such 'contributions,' their very readiness to indulge such claims may be a kind of self-denigration, a failure of dignity," (ibid.).

I have written herein an exposition of a culture transplanted by young and older Chinese. Yet I urge the reader to understand that this culture is not a hybridization of some superior cultural model spanning 5000 years of Chinese history. The Chinese in my study group lack the amphibolic, unstable footing characteristic of liminars who straddle two cultures, producing in themselves hybrid positioning, generating for themselves ambivalence and alienating identification (cf. Naficy 1993:167). Instead, the Chinese *claim* their cultural inheritance, recognizing that inheritance as impacting their determination and ability to function within the given world. The people in my study have no sense of being, nor desire to be, "just a little bit Chinese and a whole lot more American." They have a deeply ingrained sense of their traditions in which they find solidarity, comfort, and no need to escape the family unit or system of networks which bind them so successfully in their ways their lives operate daily. But this does not mean that we non-Chinese should try to identify the people in my study group solely on the basis of their traditional sense of culture.

Clearly there is space within the appetite for dialectics of immigration to this country (and others) and the cultural processes which ensue to resist lumping all diasporic people as liminars and hybrids. There has always been a China, and this China exists unobstructed in pentimento form inside my informants. A comparison, therefore, of the people in my study group with so many other peoples who are uprooted and displaced by new forms of nationalism, physical boundary movements, and large-scale penetration by other ethnic groups who significantly threaten the "pure" racial/cultural mix of a country is as unsatisfying and problematic as comparing the Chinese pentimento with the exilic (Iranian) palimpsest. If we use the model these people have illustrated for me, we simply cannot look at the Chinese immigrants as insecure people grasping to identify with something akin to the larger "opportunities" of Western life. Nor should we consider them to harbor the same kind of nostalgia witnessed in some exilic communities that has produced an illusory commonalty with the homeland, seeking to create through their imagination a presence of an absence. Strikingly, when I asked my Evergreen student informants if they wished to return to Taiwan (or the few other places they had lived most of their lives), the answer was a swift "No!" The students from Taiwan particularly had no desire to return for anything other than a visit; schools are much more exacting there, they told me, expecting the children to memorize and rigidly conform to the standards of the KMT administration. Memories of punishment adjudicated with a bamboo stick were one such wincing reason for desiring an American education. Another was the lack of physical education comparable to that required in the United States. Foremost in ranking their desires to remain here was the realization that they could enjoy their status of being Chinese and sharing their communal identity with a large Chinese community here, all the while selecting the best opportunities for their upward mobility.

The Chinese will and do accommodate themselves to us non-Chinese; further, they are delighted to be here living as a different kind of Chinese who, unlike their ancestors, are enjoying the opportunities they see the West has to offer them. But they have no rational reason nor feel an irrational impulsive emotion to sacrifice themselves on the altar of assimilation. Be they moralistic and pedagogic or promising and revealing, traditional Western stories often began with "Once upon a time. . ." and predictably followed a pattern. The Chinese I know, with their identity fashioned and not merely inherited, clearly have here in Houston a different beginning and unfolding.

NOTES

1. This is not unlike the common English exchange between two Americans: "Hi! How are you?" "Fine, thank you!"

2. I pointed out to the two students sitting nearest to me which of the provinces identified as being Chinese were actually Tibet. They had no knowledge of this, which gave me an opportunity to tell them about the atrocities inflicted by the communists on the Tibetans and their country. I explained, among other things, that Tibet was unlawfully invaded, that the Dalai Lama had fled to India, and the communists were using Tibet for a nuclear testing site and dumping ground. Both of them were very surprised, and I was surprised that no one had ever explained this to them.

3. I recalled with amusement the time an oil company executive living in Houston proudly told me he was really from the north of China. I had known he was born in Canton, and I asked him if his family were there in the south only a short while before they fled to Taiwan. "Yes, we've been in the south just 500 years," he replied to my astonished face.

Afterword

I was "in the field" nearly all the while I wrote this book. It was during the last month of my writing that I said my temporary good-byes so that I could spend more time textualizing the material I gathered and the interpretation I gave it. In explaining this to the students and to Jack, I endeavored to have them understand how much I appreciated their allowing me to be among them for so long and teaching me so much about Chinese culture and their sense of who they are and why they feel and believe that way.

Affection is bound to develop between the informants and the anthropologist after so much time together mutually focused on the work of creating an understanding between the two camps. So leaving was not an easy matter of just walking out the door. It was I who initiated the relationship, and it was I who terminated my time among them. And although I was dependent on them for helping me in my work, I was always frightfully aware of the functionalist role I had in representing them in this work. Functionalism (which differs from formalism by focusing less on the representational functions of language and more on the uses of language, on language as a means of establishing relations rather than as an object consisting of relations) is a solipsistic issue in critical representation (Tyler 1978:6-9). Just as Kwan in Amy Tan's novel *The Hundred Secret Senses* speaks of the multiple meanings in the Chinese language, we are reminded that the individual in functionalism has a more responsible place than he does in formalism. "What we take to be someone's intentions, purposes, plans, and attitudes are clues we use to interpret what he means. Consequently, meaning is a matter of interpretation rather than the automatic reading off of preordained word and sentence meanings. Where the formalist regards meaning as a function of the preexisting meanings of words and propositional forms which the speaker knows and the hearer recognizes, the functionalist sees meaning as a more variable phenomenon distilled out of the speaker's intentions and the hearer's interpretations," (Tyler 1978:7-8).

While linguistic considerations have had a considerable impact on my anthropological work, my conscience has also played a major role in my position among my informants. Was it really my place to pursuade Jack to teach Confucius's work and compare for him his teaching materials with those of another Chinese acquaintance of mine who relies heavily on traditional literature spanning several dynasties? Did I need to inform the Evergreen students about the communist Chinese invasion of Tibet and the resulting atrocities the communists had inflicted? Should I have agreed to be a sponsor for the Evergreen Youth Club, a position in which the students also assigned me the same "voting rights" as the Evergreen teachers in electing club officers (a position which meant I had to choose only a few among many)? The answers I have given myself to all these questions is that I responded to the opportunities presented to me at the time.

Did I cause Jack to lose face when I prevailed upon him to openly teach Confucius? Besides, could I, a non-Chinese woman be responsible for his losing face? Did my place in the classroom reach a level of importance that my opinion mattered? It seems my opinion did matter, and I credit him with being rather good-natured about introducing new materials right away. Further, he telephoned me just as I am finished writing this to say that I am missed and that he hoped I would return soon, especially for some of the particular annual events and celebrations (such as Chinese New Year). He seemed very happy with the current classroom experience and told me, "More kids are coming now. I'm teaching more traditional material from the mainland. That seems to attract their attention." In response, I told him I was certain the students appreciated his efforts.

Regarding the issue of Tibet's suffering at the hands of the communist Chinese, I'm still amazed that the students were so unaware of events there. Yet my conversation with them eventually led to some of them responding about other atrocities the communist Chinese inflict upon their own people. Some of the students were far more aware of forced abortions and infanticide as well as lack of free speech and poverty. "Yeah, when we go visit our relatives there, we take them so much stuff like television sets and compact disc players and food. They don't have *anything*! We're so much better off here!"

Bibliography

Ambrose, Yeo-chi King. "Kuan-shi and Network Building: A Sociological Interpretation," in *Dædalus*. Spring, 1991, pp. 63-84.

Arkush, R. David and Lee O. Lee, Translators and Editors. *Land Without Ghosts: Chinese Impressions of America From the Mid-Nineteenth Century to the Present*. Berkeley: University of California Press, 1989.

Ashton, Dore. *About Rothko*. New York: Oxford University Press, 1983.

Bakhtin, M.M. *Speech Genres and Other Late Essays*. Translated by Vern W. McGee. Edited by Caryl Emerson and Michael Holquist. Austin: University of Texas Press, 1986.

———— *The Dialogic Imagination: Four Essays*. Translated by Caryl Emerson and Michael Holquist. Edited by Michael Holquist. Austin: University of Texas Press, 1981.

Baldwin, James. "A Question of Identity," in *The Price of the Ticket: Collected Nonfiction 1948-1985*. New York: St. Martin's/Marek, 1985.

de Bary, William Theodore. *East Asian Civilizations: A Dialogue in Five Stages*. Cambridge: Harvard University Press, 1988.

Bernard, William S. *Chinese Newcomers in the United States: A Sample Study of Recent Immigrants and Refugees*. New York: American Immigration and Citizenship Conference, 1974.

Breslin, James E.B. *Mark Rothko: A Biography*. Chicago: The University of Chicago Press, 1993.

Chang, Pang-Mei Natasha. *Bound Feet and Western Dress*. New York: Doubleday, 1996.

Chen, Edward C.M. and Fred R. von der Mehden. *Chinese in Houston*. Houston: Houston Center for the Humanities; National Endowment for the Humanities, 1982.

163

Chow, Rey. *Writing Diaspora: Tactics of Intervention in Contemporary Cultural Studies*. Bloomington: Indiana University Press, 1993.

The Compact Oxford English Dictionary, 2d ed. Oxford: Clarendon Press, 1991.

Crapanzano, Vincent. *Tuhami, Portrait of a Moroccan*. Chicago: University of Chicago Press, 1980. Reference made by Tyler in *The Unspeakable: Discourse, Dialogue, and Rhetoric in the Postmodern World*, 1987, p. 66.

Dirlik, Arif. *Anarchism in the Chinese Revolution*. Berkeley: University of California Press, 1991.

——— *Revolution and History: The Origins of Marxist Historiography in China, 1919-1937*. Berkeley: University of California Press, 1978.

The Economist. London: January 21, 1995, pp. 38-39.

Fei Xiaotong. *From the Soil: The Foundations of Chinese Society*. From *Xiangtu Zhongguo*. Translated by Gary G. Hamilton and Wang Zheng. Berkeley: University of California Press, 1992.

——— "The Shallowness of Cultural Tradition," in *Land Without Ghosts: Chinese Impressions of America From the Mid-Nineteenth Century to the Present*. Translated and Edited by R. David Arkush and Leo O. Lee. Berkeley: University of California Press, 1989.

Financial Times. London: January 8, 1996, p. 18.

First Colony Magazine. Published by Sugarland Properties Incorporated, Sugar Land, Texas, 1995.

Fischer, Michael M.J. "Ethnicity and the Post-Modern Arts of Memory," in *Writing Culture: The Poetics and Politics of Ethnography*. Edited by James Clifford and George E. Marcus. Berkeley: University of California Press, 1986.

Funk & Wagnalls. *Standard College Dictionary*. New York: Harcourt, Brace & World, Inc., 1963.

Gallop, Jane. *Reading Lacan*. Ithaca: Cornell UP, 1985. Reference made by Naficy in "The Poetics and Practice of Iranian Nostalgia in Exile," 1991, p. 285.

Gergen, Kenneth J. *The Saturated Self: Dilemmas of Identity in Contemporary Life*. New York: Basic Books, 1991.

Hall, Stuart. "New Ethnicities," in *ICA Documents*. London: 1988; No. 7, pp. 27-31. Reference made by Naficy in *The Making of Exile Cultures: Iranian Television in Los Angeles*, 1993, p. 17.

Harper's Weekly. January 22, 1870. Vol. 14, No. 682, p. 53.

Hegel, Robert E. "An Exploration of the Chinese Literary Self," in *Expressions of Self in Chinese Literature*. Edited by Robert E. Hegel and Richard C. Hessney. New York: Columbia University Press, 1985.

Heidegger, Martin. "The Question Concerning Technology," in *Basic Writings*. New York: Harper Collins, 1977.

———— ". . .Poetically Man Dwells. . . ," in *Poetry, Language, Thought*. New York: Harper & Row, 1971.

Howe, Irving. *World of Our Fathers*. New York: Schocken Books, Inc. 1989.

Hsu, Francis L.K. *Americans and Chinese: Passage to Differences*, 3rd ed., Honolulu: University Press of Hawaii, 1981.

———— *Americans and Chinese: Two Ways of Life*. New York: Henry Scchuman, 1953. Reference made by Pye in *The Spirit of Chinese Politics*, 1992, p. 96.

Hu, Hsien-chin. "The Chinese Concept of Face," in *American Anthropologist*, 46, 1944, pp. 45-64. Reference made by Pye in *The Spirit of Chinese Politics*, 1992, p. 96.

Kingston, Maxine Hong. *The Woman Warrior: Memoirs of a Girlhood Among Ghosts*. New York: Vintage Books, 1989.

———— *China Men*. New York: Alfred A. Knopf, Inc., 1980.

Klineberg, Stephen L. *Houston's Ethnic Communities*, 3rd ed. Houston: Rice University, Department of Sociology, 1996.

Kristoff, Nicholas and Sheryl WuDunn. *China Wakes: The Struggle for the Soul of a Rising Power*. New York: Times Books, 1994.

Lee, Rose Hum. *The Chinese in the United States of America*. Hong Kong: Hong Kong University Press, 1960.

Liang Qichao. "The Power and Threat of America," in *Land Without Ghosts: Chinese Impressions of America From the Mid-Nineteenth Century to the Present*. Translated and Edited by R. David Arkush and Leo O. Lee. Berkeley: University of California Press, 1989.

Mc Cunn, Ruthanne Lum. *Chinese American Portraits: Personal Histories 1928-1988*. San Francisco: Chronicle Books, 1988.

de Menil, Dominique. "The Rothko Chapel," in *Art Journal*. Vol 30, No. 2, Spring, 1971, pp. 249-251.

Merlau-Ponty, Maurice. *Signs*. Translated by Richard C. McCleary. Evanston, Illinois: Northwestern University Press, 1964. Reference made by Tyler in *The Said and the Unsaid*, 1978, p. 83.

Naficy, Hamid. *The Making of Exile Cultures: Iranian Television in Los Angeles*. Minneapolis: University of Minnesota Press, 1993.

——— "The Poetics and Practice of Iranian Nostalgia in Exile," in *Diaspora*. Vol. 1, No. 3, 1991.

Naipaul, V.S. *A Way in the World*. New York: Alfred A. Knopf, 1994.

———*India: A Million Mutinies Now*. New York: Penguin Books, 1990.

The New York Times. New York: March 12, 1995, p. A1.

Pan, Lynn. *Sons of the Yellow Emperor: A History of the Chinese Diaspora*. New York: Kodansha America, Inc. 1994.

Pan, Zhongdang, Steven H. Chaffee, Godwin C. Chu, and Yanan Ju. *To See Ourselves: Comparing Traditional Chinese and American Cultural Values*. Boulder: Westview Press, 1994.

Pye, Lucien W. *The Spirit of Chinese Politics*. Cambridge: Harvard University Press, 1992.

———with Mary W. Pye. *Asian Power and Politics: The Cultural Dimensions of Authority*. Cambridge: The Belknap Press of Harvard University Press, 1985.

Reich, Robert B. *The Work of Nations: Preparing Ourselves for 21st-Century Capitalism*. New York: Alfred A. Knopf, 1991.

Ricour, Paul. *The Reality of the Historical Past*. Milwaukee: Marquette University Press, 1984.

Rorty, Richard. *Philosophy and the Mirror of Nature*. Princeton: Princeton University Press, 1979.

Said, Edward W. *Orientalism*. New York: Vintage Books, 1979.

———*Orientalism*. New York: Pantheon, 1978. Reference made by Tyler in *The Unspeakable: Discourse, Dialogue, and Rhetoric in the Postmodern World*, p. 65.

Schirokauer, Conrad. *Modern China and Japan: A Brief History*. New York: Harcourt Brace Jovanovich, Inc. 1982.

Sennett, Richard. *The Conscience of the Eye: The Design and Social Life of the Cities*. New York: Alfred A. Knopf, 1990.

Simpson, D.P. *Cassell's Latin Dictionary*. New York: Macmillan Publishing Company, 1968.

Siu, Paul C.P. *The Chinese Laundryman: A Study of Social Isolation*. New York: New York University Press, 1987.

Smith, Richard J. *China's Cultural Heritage: The Qing Dynasty, 1644-1912*, 2d ed. Boulder: Westview Press, 1994.

Spence, Jonathan D. *God's Chinese Son: The Taiping Heavenly Kingdom of Hong Xiuquan*. New York: W.W. Norton & Company, 1996.

Stevens, Christine A. "The Illusion of Social Inclusion: Cambodian Youth in South Australia," in *Diaspora*. Vol. 4., No. 5, 1995, pp. 59-76.

Sung, Betty Lee. *Mountain of Gold: The Story of the Chinese in America*. New York: The Macmillan Company, 1967.

Tan, Amy. *The Hundred Secret Senses*. New York: G. P. Putnam's Sons, 1995.

Tannen, Deborah. *Gender and Discourse*. New York: Oxford University Press, 1994.

Tyler, Stephen A. *The Unspeakable: Discourse, Dialogue, and Rhetoric in the Postmodern World*. Madison: The University of Wisconsin Press, 1987.

———"Post-Modern Ethnography: From Document of the Occult to Occult Document," in *Writing Culture: The Poetics and Politics of Ethnography*. Edited by James Clifford and George E. Marcus. Berkeley: University of California Press, 1986.

———*The Said and the Unsaid: Mind, Meaning, and Culture*. New York: Academic Press, Inc., 1978.

Wachman, Alan M. *Taiwan: National Identity and Democratization*. Armonk, New York: M. E. Sharpe, 1994.

Wang Gungwu. "Among Non-Chinese," in *Dædalus*, Spring, 1991, pp. 135-157.

Wang, L. Ling-chi. "Roots and Changing Identity of the Chinese in the United States," in *Dædalus*, Spring, 1991; pp. 181-206.

Williams, Robin M., Jr., *American Society: A Sociological Interpretation*, 3rd ed. New York: Alfred A. Knopf, 1970. Reference made by Pan, Chaffee, et. al. in *To See Ourselves: Comparing Chinese and American Cultural Values*, 1994, p. 233.

Wittgenstein, Ludwig. *Tractatus logico-philosophicus*. London: Routledge & Kegan Paul, 1922. Reference made by Tyler in *The Said and the Unsaid: Mind, Meaning, and Culture*, 1978, p. 5.

Wu, David Yen-ho. "The Construction of Chinese and Non-Chinese Identities," in *Dædalus*, Spring, 1991, pp. 159-179.

Yang, Belle. *Baba: A Return to China Upon My Father's Shoulders*. New York: Harcourt Brace & Company, 1994.

Index